# CHRISTMAS MAGIC

## THE ART OF MAKING
## DECORATIONS & ORNAMENTS

# CHRISTMAS MAGIC

## THE ART OF MAKING
## DECORATIONS & ORNAMENTS

☆ ☆ ☆

### Margaret Perry

PHOTOGRAPHS AND DRAWINGS BY THE AUTHOR

DOUBLEDAY & COMPANY, INC., GARDEN CITY, NEW YORK
1964

# ACKNOWLEDGMENTS

To *Flower Grower, the Home Garden Magazine,* for allowing me to use again some of the ideas created expressly for that publication; to Dolf and Sigrid Swing for letting me take many photographs at their Connecticut country home; and to my family and friends for their interest and inspiration I give my sincere thanks.

# CONTENTS

# LIST OF COLOR ILLUSTRATIONS

# INTRODUCTION

Christmas is a magic time, a time for reverie and reverence, fun and frolic, a time to look forward to and a time to look back upon. Christmas is a magic time all around the world.

Each corner of the globe has its own way of celebrating the holidays. And every city round the world, like a star in the earth's crown, sparkles in its own way, a little special in its traditions, its kinds of decorations, its tributes to the holiday season. Every family, in turn, has its own way of expressing the holiday mood—its particular preferences for decorating the Christmas tree, the wreath, the fireside.

To make Christmas really your own, you must create in your own special way. The symbols are universal—the tree, angels, candles, wreaths, stars, bells. Your own interpretations of these traditional symbols of the holiday season give a distinction to your celebration of Christmas.

Start with one idea, perhaps one you've seen or been told about, and before the idea is completed it will be a little different, a little individual, just a bit more personal—your own way of doing it. And as you go along, one idea will lead to another, until you'll find there are so many lovely things to do and make you won't know where to stop.

Before you begin your decorations, decide upon an over-all plan, a particular color scheme, a theme to which variations can be added, so that there will be a continuity to your accomplishments. Choose, as the Chinese do, a motif for the year—make it, perhaps, the year of the angel, or the year of the star—and decide ahead of time what colors you'd especially like to have. The year of the angel might be gold and silver, for instance, and the year of the tiny trees green and blue. Don't limit your decorations to the single motif, but make it dominant.

Tradition is the foundation of the Christmas holiday season. We all have our special collection of treasures that make up a part of the tradition for us—the crimson Santa, the golden star that has always hung just *so* on the tree. Each year these treasures are carefully packed away when the holiday is over, to be taken out of their wrappings, with fond thoughts and many memories, when the season comes round again. Add some of your creations to your collection of treasures. Start your own "traditions" and add to them as the years go by.

Christmas never comes quickly enough when we are young. Remember how we used to say, "Wait a minute, I'm coming," and the impatient playmate would call, "So is Christmas!" But as we grow older Christmas comes all too quickly and often catches us unawares. If we make December the holiday month, as our Scandinavian friends do, and begin our preparations early, we'll be ready for the festive days that start with Christmas Eve.

# CHRISTMAS MAGIC

## THE ART OF MAKING
## DECORATIONS & ORNAMENTS

☆

# CHAPTER I

# DECORATING DOORWAYS

Christmas Eve—the magic hour has come, and the world is full of carolers and candles. Warm welcomes wait at every door, and every door is decorated.

Your doorway gives a greeting to your guests and sends a warm glow out upon the winter landscape. The decorations you choose should reflect the mood of the household, be it modern and bright or completely traditional. Colors in themselves can reflect the modern mood—chartreuse, pale blue, crimson. Red and green with gold or silver, regardless of the design, give the traditional touch.

If your doorway is protected from the weather, you can choose from many materials the ones that suit you best. If wind and rain and snow and sleet will beat upon your windowpane, use plant materials and plastic ribbon for your outside decorations.

Inside doors can be decorated too. And the children of the family love their own doorway décor, especially if they make it themselves. Hall doors and kitchen doors, doors throughout the house—each can be decorated to reflect the décor found within.

## DOUBLE CORNUCOPIA

A double cornucopia holds a doorway bouquet of greens. Make it of gold or silver foil, or carry out your color scheme by using bright Christmas wrapping paper. Use two colors if you like—mine is blue on the outside and green on the inside.

### Start with a Square

Fasten together two 24-inch squares of paper, wrong sides together, by dotting one sheet very lightly with glue (Elmer's or Sobo). If you use much it will show, so use very little glue.

Make a pencil mark on the bottom edge of the paper 10 inches in from the left-hand corner. Using this mark as a guide, form a cone by rolling up the left-hand corner; hold it in place with glue or cellophane tape (or both, to make it very secure). Then form a cone from the right-hand bottom corner and

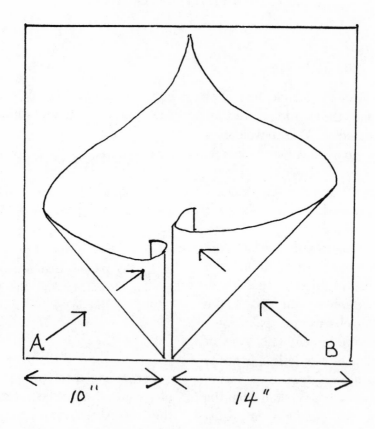

A

B

10″

14″

secure it in the same fashion. Make sure the points of both cones are exactly side by side.

Trim off the top of the sheet as shown in the accompanying diagram, and attach to a door with a thumbtack.

Fill both cornucopias with ever-greens. Long-needled pine and holly are especially good to use, because they will last a long time without water. I added a few sprays of juniper. The red holly berries and the bluish-gray juniper berries make a lovely color combination.

## FUNNEL BELLS

Your kitchen door plays an important part in the holiday festivities. Through this doorway come all the goodies for the Christmas parties, the turkeys and hams, the fruits and vegetables, the finest food for family and friends that adds so much to the joy of the festive season.

There are many ways to decorate the kitchen door. These golden bells are made of ordinary kitchen funnels strung on golden cord.

Three 2½-inch funnels (about fifteen cents each at any hardware or dime store) are covered with gold paint or spray. For the bottom bell I used a piece of gold cord about 16 inches long.

I tied a small (1-inch) Christmas ball in the center of the piece of cord, made a large knot about an inch above the ball so it would hang down inside the bell like a clapper, and then ran the double cord up through the funnel. I used about 14 inches of cord for the middle bell, and 12 inches for the top one, and made clappers of Christmas balls in each.

This cluster of bells is not only simple to make, it is quick as well, especially if you use a fast-drying gold paint. By the time you have finished painting the third bell, the first is ready to be fitted with a clapper.

Attach the bells to a branch of evergreens (I used long-needled pine) and hang the spray on the kitchen door.

## METALLIC-FOIL BELLS

A cluster of bells tied to your doorway with evergreen branches will ring in the Christmas season.

Use metallic foil for these, and they will withstand the weather, at least for one season.

### Start with a Circle

For every two bells, cut a circle 5 inches in diameter. Using half the circle, staple to form a cone, catching in the staple one end of a 15-inch piece of gold cord (available at any notion counter). Let the cord go through the point of the cone.

Make five or seven or as many bells as you like, and tie them together in a cluster. Attach them to sprays of evergreen with very fine wire, and hang on the door.

These bells are effective not only on a doorway but tied to the railing of your porch or outside stairway—or on a balcony railing, as shown here. Again you can mix the colors or make them all of gold or silver.

If you want the bells to predominate, be sparing of the greens. Choose an interestingly shaped branch of long-needled pine for an airy effect.

## SLEIGH-BELL *KLOCKASTRÄNG*

In Scandinavia *klockasträngs* (bell pulls) are popular for doorway decorations at Christmas time. Traditionally, the *klockasträng* carried a cowbell— a bell that was available at every farm and village. Tied with ribbons and hung with greens, the bell was rung by visitors to announce their arrival. Today the cowbell is still used, and almost always it is painted gold.

The *klockasträng* shown here is made in the traditional style of strips of felt, sleigh bells, and a gold-painted cowbell.

### Start with a Strip

Use green, red, and white felt—green for the background, white in the middle, and red on top. The green strips (there are three of each color) are 2½ inches wide, the red is 2 inches wide, and the white is 1½ inches wide.

Cut the strips with pinking scissors. The longest ones are 18, 17½, and 17 inches long; the middle ones 15, 14½, and 14 inches long; and the shortest ones are 12, 11½, and 11 inches long. Taper the ends to points.

Sew on sleigh bells right through the three thicknesses in a row, as I have, or in clusters.

Attach the three pulls to a ring— either wood, as here, or wire—using a heavy needle and strong thread. On a separate strip of red felt, hang the cowbell in the center.

Hang the *klockasträng* on your door with a spray of evergreens, and your friends and neighbors will let you know that they have arrived by ringing the cowbell. The sleigh bells will jingle too.

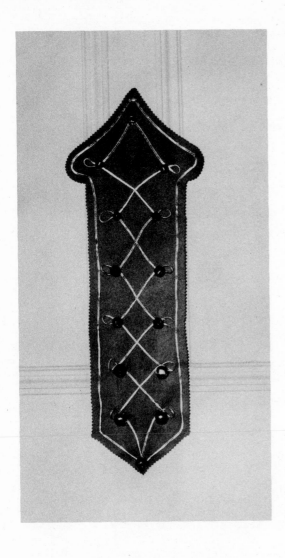

## RED FELT *KLOCKASTRÄNG*

Made especially for your own door and made from your own design, a *klockasträng* has a great deal of charm. Here's one made of red felt, gold braid, and sleigh bells.

### Start with a Strip

This strip is 23 inches long and 9 inches wide. To decorate the *klockasträng* you will need about 3 yards of gold braid and fourteen sleigh bells of different colors. Before cutting the felt, cut a pattern out of newspaper.

To make the pattern, fold a large sheet of newspaper in half. With a soft pencil, draw *half* of the design you have decided on, using the fold as the center line. Cut the pattern, open it up—and if the design doesn't suit you, try again!

When you have a design you like, place the pattern on the felt and cut with pinking scissors.

Attach gold braid to the felt either by sewing it on or by using glue. I prefer the glue because it is much quicker, but on the other hand, you do have to be very careful not to let any show beyond the braid. Even the milky glues that dry clear will leave a slight spot on colored felt. If you do use glue, use very little and apply with a toothpick.

Sew on sleigh bells at the points where the braid crosses, and sew on one at the center top and another at the center bottom.

Fasten the top of the *klockasträng* to your door with a thumbtack or brass-headed nail, leaving the bottom free so that your visitors can take hold of it to sound the bells on their arrival.

7

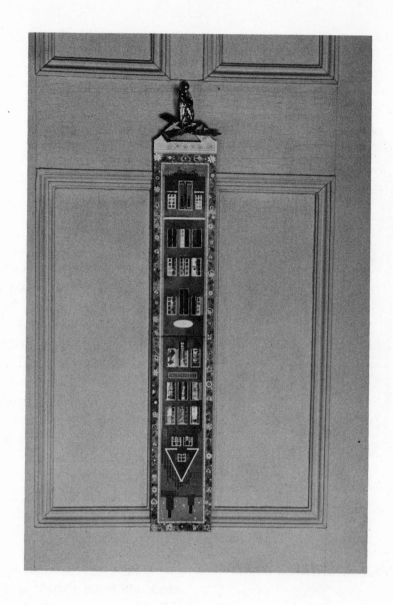

## DANISH *KLOCKASTRÄNG*

This *klockasträng* comes from Denmark and serves two purposes: It announces the visitor with a jingle of bells, and it announces the approaching holiday with the opening of its little windows and doors, thus serving as an Advent calendar.

There is a window or a door for each day of December, from the first to Christmas Eve. Each morning the shutter for that date is opened, revealing scenes of activity in preparation for the holiday season, until finally, on the twenty-fourth, the last window is opened—and there is the Christmas tree.

In the close-up of the *klockasträng* you can see how each window is dated

8

and how the little shutters open. In the first window shown in the close-up, the window dated the sixteenth, one finds the family cook busily making Christmas cakes; in the next are two Christmas *tomtes* (elves) singing carols.

Some of the shutters are decorated with pots of bright flowers, some with designs using the heart—a favorite design in Scandinavia at Christmas time.

A bright border edges the *klockasträng* and a cluster of bells is tied at the bottom.

Fasten to your doorway with a thumbtack at the top—an inside doorway, of course, because even though the paper used is heavy, it will not withstand the weather. For directions on how to make your own Advent *klockasträng*, see the chapter on Christmas cards.

## DOORKNOB DECOR

Decorate your doorknob with a "keyhole" cut from felt. Choose your colors and your design to harmonize with the other decorations on your door. And remember that the knob itself is functional and should be left free. Also, your design must not be so wide that it will interfere with the closing of the door. The placement of knobs varies, so fit your décor to your door.

Cut a pattern out of newspaper, following the diagrams given, for each of the pieces. I used green felt for the star-shaped piece, and this one I cut with regular scissors. It is about 9 inches long and 6 inches wide—which was about right for my door. For the second piece

I used white felt, and cut it with pinking scissors. The white piece is 7½ inches long and 3½ inches wide.

Place the white piece carefully on the green, centering it, and secure it with a few dots of glue.

Find the center of the circular (or top) part of the "keyhole" and mark it with a pencil. From this center point cut eight slits about ¾ inch long, through both layers of felt, so that the doorknob can be slipped through.

Edge with gold braid, glued on, and three gold sleigh bells sewed across the bottom through both layers.

Reverse the pattern if you like, cutting the white piece in the shape of a many-pointed star. Decorate with gold braid and sew the bells in a row down the middle.

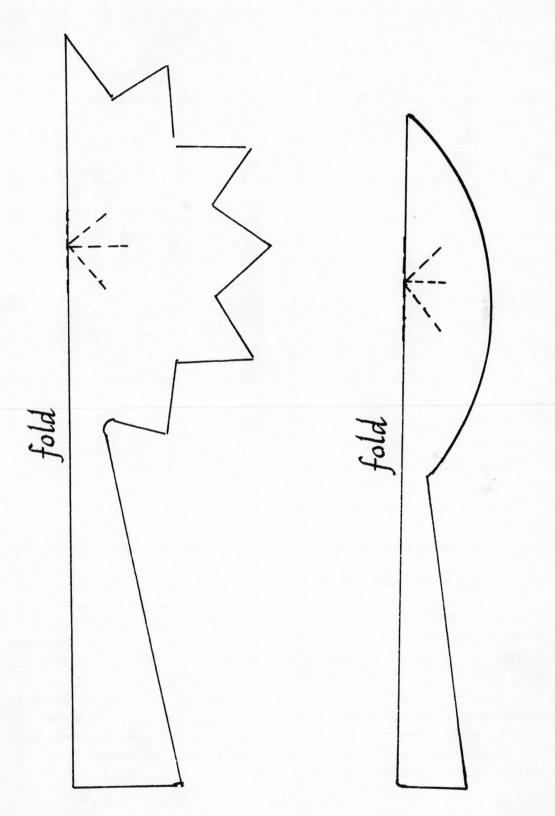

fold

fold

11

## TREASURE *KLOCKASTRÄNG*

Here is a *klockasträng* that has become a family tradition, a treasure that has grown with the years.

### Start with a Strip

The strip is red felt, 20 inches long and 3 inches wide, cut out with pinking scissors. A dark-green inch-wide satin ribbon is sewn down through the middle of the red felt. On this ribbon are attached bells and buttons of particular significance—a bell from a daughter's favorite party costume, crystal buttons from a special dress, the square wooden buttons that brightened a wool jacket—each one bringing, year by year, another decoration to the doorpull.

Winding its way down among the baubles is a narrow gold cord, circling at the bottom a single, sizable sleigh bell that had been worn by the daughter on her shoe in Morris dances during her school days. The family initial —S—on an ivory button finishes the strand.

## ORANGE-JUICE-CAN BELLS

The traditional Christmas colors—red, green, and gold—are used for this doorway swag, bringing brilliance and beauty to the back door.

The bells are made of frozen-orange-juice cans from which the tops have been completely removed. Cover the cans with gold paint (they'll probably need two coats), and punch a hole in the bottom of each can with a can opener or screw driver.

Run a wide (2 inches at least) red satin ribbon through each hole, knotting one end so that the can won't slip off. Tie the three bells together in such a way that each one hangs a little below the next, and attach to a big red bow and a bough of evergreens.

☆

# CHAPTER II

# TABLES AND TREES

Nothing quite symbolizes Christmas for us as appropriately as does a tree. It is the focal point of festivities for most of us, the symbol of the season, especially for the children.

Table trees can be made in all shapes and sizes and of many different kinds of materials, from tiny trees of tissue paper to 2-foot-tall trees made of plant material. And in general, of course, the smallest table takes the littlest tree.

Tables take on significance, too, during the holiday season, for it is our tables that we decorate for all the Christmas parties—buffet tables, dining tables, hall tables, coffee tables, all kinds of tables large and small.

We all have our favorite ways of trimming our tables and trees. Here are some of mine.

## KNITTING-NEEDLE TREE

The knitting-needle tree is a glamorous one that can be used for the hall table, the mantel, or as a centerpiece for the dining table. For this tree you can mix your colors or keep them within a color scheme.

Start with a knitting needle 14 inches long. Be sure it is the kind that has a metal cap at the blunt end to keep the stitches from falling off. String four large Christmas balls (each about 4 inches in diameter) onto the needle, slipping the little metal loops on the balls over the point of the needle. These four balls will form the base of the tree, and if you place them squarely on a table, they will hold the needle upright.

Next, string onto the needle four balls of a slightly smaller size. Each one will fit between two of the larger ones. Then string on another four, slightly smaller, and finally four more, again slightly smaller, so that your tree has sixteen Christmas balls in all. On the top of the needle place a Christmas-tree peak.

If you want to move the tree, take off the peak and pick up the tree by the point of the knitting needle.

Experiment with your colors. Try a different color for each size—say, red, green, blue, and gold—or try four balls

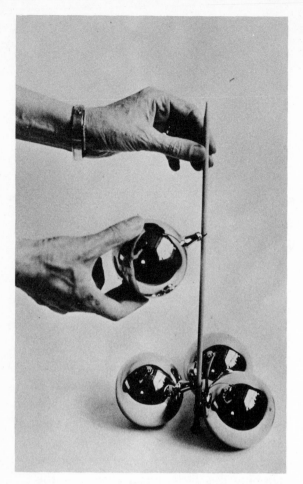

of varying sizes in each color. This can give you a spiral effect. Sometimes I make mine entirely of silver and combine it with silver candlesticks holding red candles.

Decorate the base of the tree with evergreens or holly or place it on a Christmas centerpiece made of felt, which you will find at the end of this chapter.

## SNOWBALL TREE

The snowball tree was made especially as the centerpiece for a children's party. Surrounded by snowman place cards and decorated with sprigs of evergreen, it makes a most appealing setting.

The base of the tree is a 10-inch

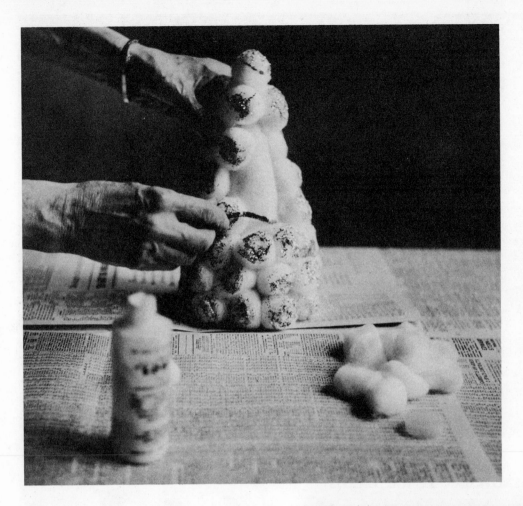

Styrofoam cone (or make a cone of cardboard). Cotton balls—the kind that come packaged in cellophane for applying and removing cosmetics—make the tree.

Dip each cotton ball in a bit of glue and then in silver glitter, just one side of the ball. Then, starting at the bottom of the cone, glue the cotton balls in place, putting the last one on the point of the cone.

To add sparkle to the tree, glue a tiny silver Christmas ball (½ inch in diameter) into the space between the cotton balls.

The finished tree is fluffy and snowy, and it's icy-looking too.

## SNOWMAN PLACE CARDS

The snowman is made by gluing two cotton balls together. Before gluing, compress the top one by rolling it between the palms of your hands, so that the snowman's head is a bit smaller than his body. Tie a piece of gold cord or colored ribbon around the neck.

For the hat, cut a circle of metallic foil (or colored construction paper) 1¼ inches in diameter. For the crown, cut a strip 1¼ inches by 2¼ inches, roll it up by gluing the short ends together, and attach to the center of the circle with glue. Another touch of glue will hold it to the snowman's head.

Attach the snowman, with glue, to a 2-inch by 3-inch card made of the same color and material as the hat.

Cut out of snapshots the face of each child invited to the party and paste each picture to a snowman. This, of course, requires the cooperation of all the mothers, but it is worth the effort just to watch the youngsters' glee when they find their faces on the snowmen.

Snowman place cards are fun for family parties too, for children and grownups alike.

[1] The Christmas village is assembled under the Christmas tree on a snowy landscape of cotton. For instructions see Chapter IV.

[2] Wall sconce of aluminum made in the shape of a Christmas tree shines like pewter in the candlelight. See Chapter III.

[3] To hang on the wall or stand on a table, aluminum sconce can be made in many different shapes, including the fleur-de-lis. For instructions for making sconces, see Chapter III.

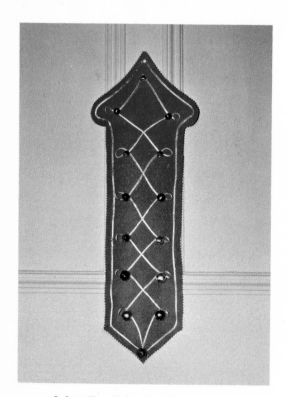

[4] Bell pull for the door is made of red felt and trimmed with sleigh bells and gold braid. Instructions are in Chapter I.

[5] Sconce in the triptych form is made of aluminum to stand on a table. For complete directions, see Chapter III.

[6] The copper angel holds her candles to light up the Swedish *rosmåling* plate. Instructions for making the angel are given in Chapter III.

[7] Angel ring trimmed with princess pine hangs over the party buffet. Instructions are given in Chapter VII.

[8] Holly and a small blueberry branch are arranged with birds on a pewter plate. See Chapter VI.

[9] A big red bow and a cluster of foil bells decorate a doorway. Directions for making the bells are given in Chapter I.

[10] A mobile made of five paper birds in contrasting colors is made on copper wire. Instructions are given in Chapter VIII.

[11] A green felt mat, trimmed with golden braid and sequins, protects the coffee table. Instructions are given in Chapter II.

[13] A candle on a liqueur glass brightens the cookie tray. See Chapter III.

[12] Goblets are turned into candlesticks, with bright Christmas balls inside. See Chapter III.

## GLITTER TREE

Trees covered with glitter add brightness to a table by reflecting the light from Christmas candles. Use them to trim a party table or in the Christmas village.

### Start with a Circle

Make a cone of one third of a 10-inch circle of green construction paper, stapling it together. Cover the cone with Sobo glue and roll it in glitter that has been scattered on a newspaper.

Snip off the point of the cone (no more than ⅛ inch) and insert a small Christmas ball on a pipe cleaner. If you have used silver glitter, use a silver Christmas ball—gold glitter with a gold ball. Or use a green Christmas ball to match the green cone base, which will show through the glitter.

## ESPALIER TREE

The traditional espaliered pear tree enhances a hall table at Christmas time. It is particularly appealing if it has a partridge sitting in it.

This pear tree is 16 inches high and is made of five pieces of wire. For the center stem cut a piece of 14-gauge wire 16 inches long. Then cut two pieces of 18-gauge wire (this is not quite so heavy) 19 inches long for the two lower branches and two pieces of 18-gauge wire 18 inches long for the upper branches.

The lower right-hand branch is twisted, starting at the bottom, around the center stem to a point 7½ inches up the stem; then it is bent out at right angles for 5½ inches and up for 5½ inches. The lower left-hand branch is attached in the same way.

The upper right-hand branch is twisted around the main stem, starting at the bottom, to a point 10½ inches up from the bottom, then bent out for 3½ inches and up for 3 inches. The upper left-hand branch is then attached in the same way.

Cut long strips of green crepe paper (about an inch wide) and wrap around all stems, securing with a touch of glue.

Next, wire on as many miniature artificial pears as you like—I used fourteen for mine. These fruits are available in handcraft and hobby shops and in five-and-ten-cent stores, as are the leaves. When the fruits are in place, wire on the leaves, placing them so that they will conceal wires of the fruit.

Fasten espalier in container (I used a 3-inch plastic flower pot painted gold, but you can also use ceramic or pottery) with plastic modeling clay or floral clay.

The partridge for the pear tree is made of metallic foil, with wings and tail of the metallic-foil fringe available in all dime stores at Christmas time. Cut two pieces of foil for the body, following the pattern given. Glue pieces of fringe between the two bodies, making the tail feathers longer than the wings. Attach to the pear tree with double-faced cellophane tape.

26

## TREE OF DRIED BLOSSOMS

For table decorations, for favors at your Christmas party, for color in your Christmas village—tiny trees of dried blossoms have many uses.

*Start with a Circle*

Use construction paper or lightweight cardboard. A circle 7 inches in diameter will make three trees. Cut the circle into thirds and staple each third to form a cone.

Starting at the bottom of the cone, I carefully placed dried blossoms of red- and gold-colored strawflowers so that the colors would be mixed evenly, attaching the flowers with a touch of Sobo glue and topping the tree with one red blossom.

The whole process took me quite a long time, and when the tree was finished a friend of mine, who had been watching me, looked askance at the clock. "I have five children coming home from school," she said, "and my husband will arrive on the six twenty-nine. Dinner guests are coming, and I need just such tiny trees for my table. But I haven't much time."

She cut a circle, made a cone with one third of it, smeared it with glue, and rolled it in the dried blossoms, which she had scattered on a newspaper. In no time she had her tree—you can judge for yourself from the photograph which one appeals to you. The "quickie" is on the left.

Three tiny Danish *tomtes*—they are made of wood and their caps are painted red, so that the colors blend well with the gold and red blossoms—give the tree dimension.

## SEGMENTED PAPER TREE

When you make a tree for your Christmas village, you can make it of green construction paper—or if your scene is snowy, you can make it of plain white bond typing paper.

### Start with a Square

For the green tree, cut four 6-inch squares. For the white tree, cut twelve squares. Both trees are made in the same way, as follows:

Fold each square in half and cut according to the pattern given. When all sections of the tree are cut, open each one flat, stack them all up, and staple three times along the crease made down through the center of the "trunk"—staple at top and bottom and in the middle. Be as careful as you can to get the staple right on the crease.

Open up the tree by gently folding each leaf until the segments are evenly spaced, and stand it up.

To keep your tree for another year, fold it flat and store it away.

If you want to make a snowy scene on a small table—perhaps in the hall or on the coffee table—place two or three cotton-ball snowmen beside the little white tree.

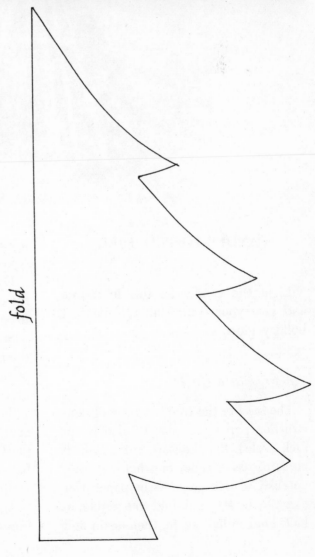

*fold*

29

## CANDLE-TOPPED TREE

Light the candle on this little tree and give your coffee table a pleasant holiday glow.

### Start with a Circle

The base of the tree is a cone of construction paper (use one third of a 12-inch circle). For the skirt, cut a 10-inch circle of tissue paper of whatever color you like (I used green tissue paper over a white cone) and fold the circle in half. Fold in half again, then again and again, until your tissue-paper circle is folded up to ½-inch segments.

Open up the circle and refold, using the creases of the first folding as a guide, in accordion-pleat fashion.

Snip off ¼ inch of the point, and slip the pleated "tree" over the construction-paper cone. Secure with a few dots of glue.

Snip off ¼ inch of the point of the cone. Into the top of the cone insert a plastic birthday-cake candleholder that has been painted gold. Add a 3-inch white candle of the nondrip type.

The candle will burn for about twenty minutes, and can easily be replaced.

## TISSUE-PAPER TREE

Dress up your party table with tissue-paper trees. They are easy to make and inexpensive too. I've made mine of pink and gold, which gives an ethereal effect.

A slender cone of construction paper, cut from a circle 12 inches in diameter, forms the base of the tree. Cut a circle of tissue paper 10 inches in diameter. Fold in half, then in half again and again, until the circle is tightly folded into ½-inch sections. Unfold, and then refold in accordion-pleated fashion, using the first creases as a guide.

Snip off the point and slip the pleated tissue paper over the cone, securing it with a dab of glue. Snip off the point of the cone and insert a small Christmas ball—one that is attached to a pipe cleaner. Glue a strip of gold braid around the top of the tree, just under the Christmas ball.

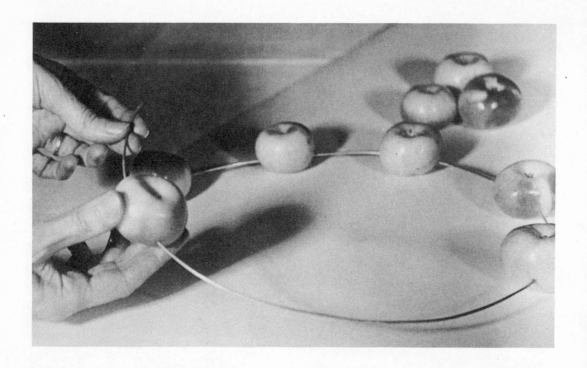

## APPLE CENTERPIECE

Apples and evergreens from your own garden will make the perfect centerpiece for your holiday dinner table.

Remove the stems of eight lady apples —or crab apples—and scoop out holes large enough for 5-inch candles. If you want your centerpiece to last through the holidays, coat the apples with a clear lacquer to prevent shriveling.

String the apples on a piece of heavy wire (14-gauge) about 38 inches long, spacing the apples evenly. Bend wire into a circle and secure both ends in one apple. You could, of course, just stand the apples in a ring. But the wire holds them securely, so that if something should bump into them they won't topple over.

Fasten the candles with a few drops of melted candle wax. Cover wire with sprigs of evergreen or strands of princess pine.

For the center, choose the largest apple you can find, scoop out the stem, and wedge a tall candle in the hole by using sprigs of evergreen.

You can achieve a color scheme to suit your holiday décor by the kind of apples you choose—red or yellow, or even green; by the kind of evergreens you use; and by the color of the candles you select. Use red apples with red or white (or both) candles and very green evergreens such as cryptomeria, white pine, balsam; use yellow apples and yellow or white candles with yellowish-green foliage; green apples and blue candles with bluish-green evergreens.

If there is a fire flickering in your fireplace, toss in a few scraps of apple peel and some twigs of evergreen—they will give a lovely aroma!

34

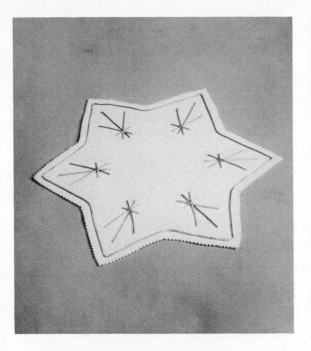

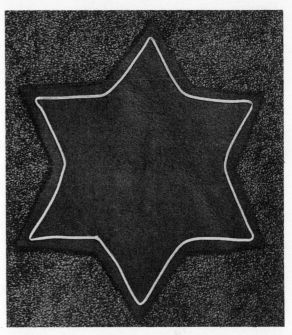

## FELT STAR-SHAPED
## CENTERPIECE

Your coffee table takes on a festive air with a Christmas-star centerpiece made of felt. And your hot coffeepot can sit right on it. Here are three to choose from. The one on the coffee table is green, the one with a Christmas star in each point is white, and the one edged with a single band of gold braid is red.

### Start with a Square

For the green mat I used a piece of felt 18 inches square. From a piece of newspaper (also 18 inches square) I cut a pattern for a six-pointed star (see page 76 for directions for making a six-pointed star). With pinking scissors I cut the star out of the green felt.

Glue gold braid around the star about ½ inch in from the edge. Be careful not to spill any glue on the felt—it will leave a mark. Decorate the corners of the star with clusters of sequins. A touch of glue with a toothpick will fasten them to the felt.

For the white felt centerpiece, start with a 14-inch square. Cut in the shape of a six-pointed star, glue gold braid around it, and decorate the corners with Christmas stars made of gold braid, tacked on with glue.

The Christmas star has four pieces— the longest (in the middle) is 3 inches long; the two shorter ones are 2½ inches long; and the crosspiece is 1 inch long.

The red centerpiece is 12 inches across, and is made in the same fashion, trimmed with one band of gold braid.

Once you have your pattern cut, the mats are quickly made. If you like to use your dining table with place mats instead of a tablecloth, make a star-shaped felt place mat for each member of the family, and use them for Christmas breakfast or midnight supper on Christmas Eve.

☆

CHAPTER III

# CANDLELIGHT

This is the time for reverence and reverie—when all the candles are lighted and the soft glow and flickering flame cast their magic spell. This is the time for peaceful thoughts and quiet conversations, a time for contemplation and contentment at the end of a bustling day.

The magic spell of candlelight is more than just myth. It softens tongues and tempers and reduces the decibels. It casts shadows and creates colors that were not there before. As the candles are lighted we pause to reflect on the fascination of the flickering flame, and before we know it we're caught in the magic mood.

Here are some suggestions for candleholders to add to your collection. Most of them can be stored away and brought out year after year.

## CHRISTMAS-TREE SCONCE

The Christmas-tree sconce for the wall over the sofa, or beside a tip-top table in a hall, or over the party buffet table is made of aluminum. When the candle is lighted the aluminum gives a soft glow like pewter.

This sconce is 7 inches high, with a 2-inch shelf to hold the candle. Cut a newspaper pattern first, following the diagram on page 38. Trace around your pattern with a pencil on a sheet of aluminum. Cut with regular household scissors and smooth the edges with sandpaper or an emery board.

Bend up the shelf of the sconce, as indicated on the diagram by the dotted line. Polish the sconce with extra-fine steel wool—very gently. This will give it the soft look of pewter.

For the candleholder, cut a piece of aluminum as shown in the sketch. Bend up the four side pieces, as indicated by the dotted lines, leaving about a square inch in the center for the candle to sit on. Attach the candleholder to the center of the shelf with Le Page's liquid solder. Let it dry overnight before you try to put a candle in it, and the bond will hold.

With a nail, make a small hole at the top of the sconce and hang it on the wall. Trim with sprigs of long-needled pine, juniper, yew, or whatever you have in your garden, light your candle—and let it cast its spell!

37

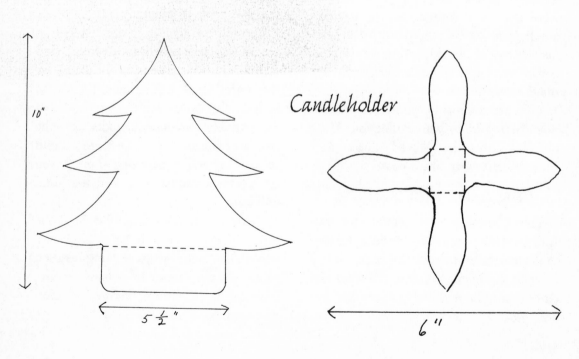

10"

5½"

*Candleholder*

6"

38

## FLEUR-DE-LIS SCONCE

The fleur-de-lis sconce is made in the same fashion as the Christmas-tree sconce. This one is 7½ inches high, with a shelf 2½ inches wide.

Using the sketch as a guide, cut a pattern of newspaper, trace it on the aluminum sheet with a pencil, and cut with scissors. Smooth the rough edges, bend up the shelf, and attach a candle-holder made like the one for the Christmas-tree sconce (see sketch).

Store your sconces away for the next Christmas season. They will soon become a tradition in your holiday décor.

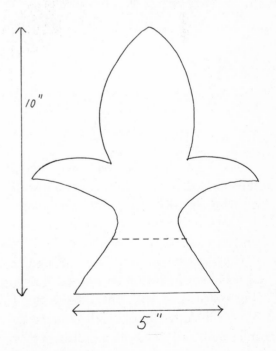

39

## TRIPTYCH SCONCE

The triptych sconce can stand on a table or a desk, or it can hang on a wall to send its triple glow into the room. It is made of aluminum just as the tree and fleur-de-lis sconces are made.

Cut a pattern of newspaper, using the sketches on following pages as a guide, and proceed as with the others. Bend along all dotted lines of the sconce as indicated, and stand it up. Polish gently with fine steel wool.

For the shelf, a separate piece of aluminum is attached, to make a smooth surface for the candleholders. Cut the shelf according to the dimensions given (draw the shelf with pencil and ruler on the aluminum first), and attach to the sconce with liquid solder, which comes ready to spread, like glue.

The candleholders for this sconce are square, as shown in the diagram. Cut according to dimensions given (again,

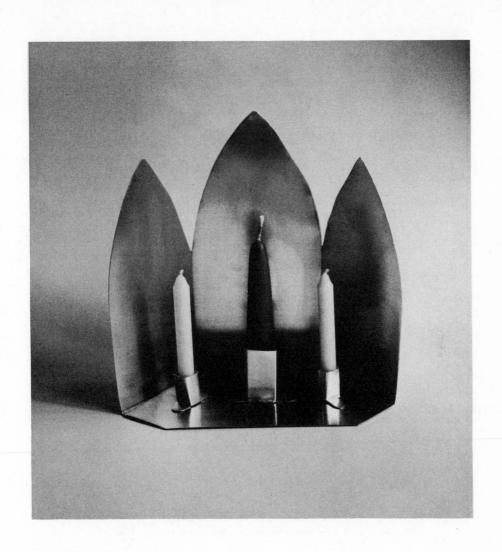

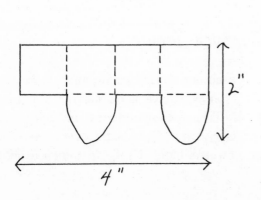

4"

2"

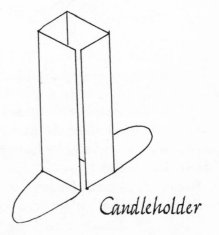

Candleholder

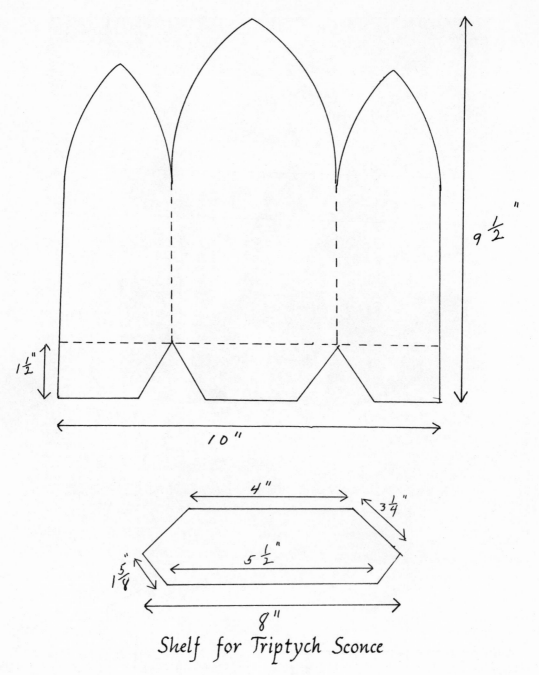

*Shelf for Triptych Sconce*

draw on aluminum with pencil and ruler first). Bend along the five dotted lines to form a candleholder like the one shown in the sketch.

Secure the candleholders on the shelf, using liquid solder, and center each one so that each panel of the triptych will have a candle in front of it.

Trim with evergreens, and light it for Christmas Eve and every eve till Twelfth-night. Use 5- or 6-inch candles.

## CANDLES AND GOBLETS

Goblets become candleholders when they are turned upside down. Stand them in a row on a wide window sill. Let them light the living room, lined up along the mantel. March them down the middle of the *smörgåsbord* table. They are bright and effective and very quick and easy to arrange.

Inside each goblet, place a large Christmas ball, each one a different color. Secure 10-inch red candles to the bottoms of the goblets (which are now the tops) with candle wax or floral clay. If you use clay, hide it with sprigs of evergreen. If you use candle wax, decorate or not as you wish—the wax matches the candle and does not show.

43

## LUCIA, THE QUEEN OF LIGHT

*Lucia Dagen,* or Lucia's Day, is celebrated in Scandinavia on the thirteenth of December to welcome in the Christmas season—the season of light.

Lucia (pronounced Loo-see'-a) is the Queen of Light. She dresses in a long white robe and wears a crown of lighted candles on her head, as she walks from room to room at dawn, carrying a tray of coffee and rolls to all the members of the family.

Traditionally, Lucia's crown contained real candles, but today the candles are electrified—like little flashlights.

In many of the offices in Scandinavia today the custom is followed. Sometime during the day, on the thirteenth of December, Lucia comes with lighted crown and a tray of rolls and coffee.

Here we have a 12-inch doll to celebrate *Lucia Dagen.* Her robe is made of white silk, and her crown holds seven 3½-inch candles. It is made on an embroidery hoop 4 inches in diameter—which just fits her head. The candles, evenly spaced, are attached with masking tape. Princess pine is wound around the hoop and held in place with very fine wire.

We rarely light her candles—unless we are watching carefully—but she stands in the hall to greet our guests as a symbol of the season of light.

45

## LUCIA CROWN

The old-fashioned Lucia crown is easier to use as a centerpiece than as a headpiece! This one came from Stockholm. The large department store in the center of Stockholm, Nordiske Kompaniet, sells these all year round. So if your travels take you to Sweden in mid-summer, you can get Lucia's crown.

The crown holds seven 5½-inch candles (the usual number) in little holders attached to an inch-wide metal band. Decorated with evergreens, it goes well on a large coffee table or as a dining-table centerpiece with a small bouquet inside the ring.

It also fits well on the head, cushioned with a white lace handkerchief. The metal band is made so that it is adjustable to fit all head sizes. But unless you have your own personal fire brigade in attendance, you'll be wiser not to light it!

## CHRISTMAS CHANDELIER

The Christmas chandelier—a traditional design in traditional colors.

Attach three 5-inch candles, equally spaced, to the outside of an 8-inch embroidery hoop, using masking tape to secure them. Tie three narrow (¼-inch) red satin ribbons to the hoop at the points where the candles are attached—ribbons about 15 inches long. Tie the ends together in a tight knot, making sure the chandelier is level. This is the hardest part of the whole job!

Princess pine is wound around the hoop and fastened with very fine wire that comes on a spool. This pine is on the conservation list in many states, but if you pick it on private property or just ahead of the bulldozer, you will be doing the pine no harm. Mine was gathered on a woodsy hillside at the home of friends in Connecticut.

Hang the chandelier from the ceiling or on a wall bracket above a buffet. For instructions on how to make the wall bracket, see the chapter on mobiles.

Light your candles *only* if your pine is very fresh and green or if it has been sprayed with a fire-deterrent spray, and *only* if you keep an eye on them. The pine burns easily when it is dry.

## WINEGLASSES AND CANDLES

Wineglasses used as candleholders have endless possibilities. They can be placed over the tiny Christmas figurines that all of us collect, giving them a showcase topped with candlelight.

Put one on your silver tray filled with Christmas cookies, with your tiniest angel shining through the glass. Try one on your cheese board, with a min-iature mouse trapped safely inside. Place one before each dinner guest, holding a partridge under the glass.

Here is a wineglass placed over a small white Christmas sprite, which stands in the center of a hand-painted Swedish *rosmåling* tray. Add crackers and cheese for the cocktail hour, or *bakkels* (Christmas cakes) to serve with afternoon sherry.

The 5-inch candle is attached with floral clay. Sprigs of evergreen trim the base of the candle.

## ANGEL RING WITH CANDLES

The combination of copper and gold gives an illusion of antiquity. Add to this the glow of candlelight and you have a luster of a very special kind.

These angels are made of copper; the ring is covered with gold braid. Each angel holds a 3½-inch white candle.

First, tie three pieces of gold braid, each about 15 inches long, to a 6-inch wooden embroidery hoop, spacing the cords evenly around the hoop. Secure with Sobo glue, and tie the ends in a

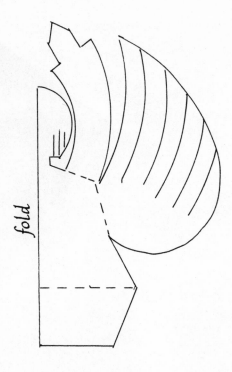

*fold*

firm knot. Make sure the ring hangs level.

Next, wind gold braid around the hoop, fastening it with glue as you go along. Take a bit of care each time you come to one of the cords that have already been tied to the hoop, smoothing the braid carefully over the knots.

Next, from a sheet of 36-gauge copper, cut out three angels, making a pattern from the one given here. (Do not fold the copper, only the pattern.) The copper cuts very easily, even with manicure scissors.

Cut along all lines on wings and head. With the points of embroidery scissors or with very small pointed pliers, roll up the strips on each side of the head to form curls.

Bend up candle shelf and bend wings back, as indicated by dotted lines on the pattern. For candleholders, cut strips of copper ½ inch wide and 1½ inches long. Roll around the candle to get the proper size, and fasten to the center of candle shelf with liquid solder.

After the solder has thoroughly dried, fasten the angels to the hoop, one between each golden cord, with Sobo glue. For extra security, run a single strand of gold cord around the hoop, letting it go between the body of the angel and the candleholder. Fasten it with glue.

Place candles in the candleholders, fold arms down around candles—and your angel ring is complete.

## ANGEL
## HOLDING TWO CANDLES

This angel can be made of either copper or aluminum. The copper is easier to cut, but on the other hand, the aluminum is sturdier and much less likely to be dented. Once having fashioned an aluminum angel, you'll have her for many a year.

The color, of course, will be quite different, depending on whether you choose copper or aluminum—one has a luster and the other a silvery gleam.

Use the pattern given here, and trace around it on the metal with a pencil. If you use aluminum, cut with household scissors. And remember that rough or jagged edges can be smoothed out with sandpaper. If you use copper, cut with embroidery scissors.

Cut all lines on wings and head. Roll curls forward and down toward the face. Carefully turn the disks that hold the candles so they are horizontal. Bend arms and wings as indicated by dotted lines on the pattern and bend the skirt to form a cone.

Cut strips of metal, ¾ inch by ½ inch, and curl them around the candle to get the proper size. Attach them to the disks with liquid solder.

The candles will burn for only twenty minutes, but they are easily replaced.

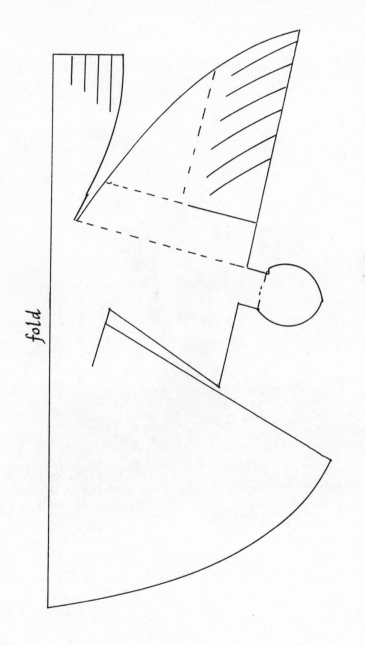

fold

## ANGEL
### HOLDING A SINGLE CANDLE

This angel, too, can be made of copper or of aluminum. Cut according to the pattern given and cut all lines on wings and head. Bend along dotted lines. Roll the curls forward and down toward the face. Fasten a circle of metal between the hands to hold the candle. I use a 3½-inch candle for this one.

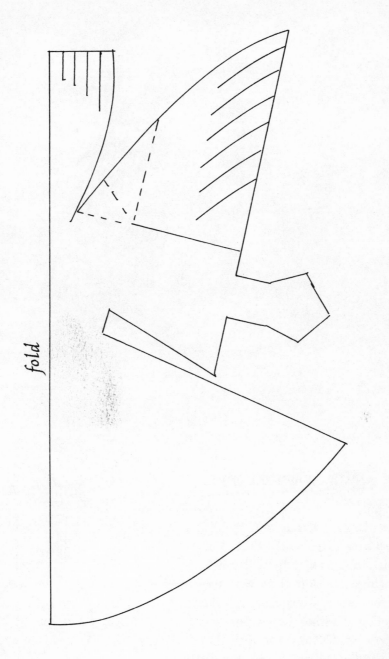

fold

55

## COPPER ANGEL WITH CANDLE

This circular angel, cut out of copper, carries a candle on her skirt. Follow the pattern given. You will notice that the wings are slotted so that one fits into the other, thus holding the angel together. Feather her wings and roll up her curls. Cut out the disk that holds the candle, following the pattern given. Bend it up along dotted line and fasten it to the skirt at the shaded area in the sketch. Use liquid solder. Cut a ½-inch strip large enough to go

### Candleholder

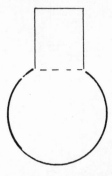

around the base of a 3½-inch candle and secure it to the disk. Bend arms down around the candle.

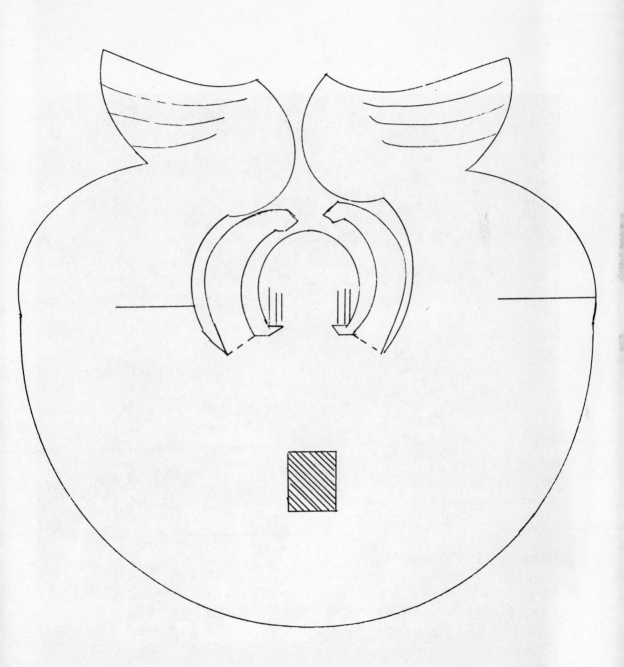

☆

# CHAPTER IV

# THE CHRISTMAS VILLAGE

When you are planning your Christmas decorations, you will want to include a Christmas village to symbolize peace and good will, a tranquil setting in a wintry landscape inhabited by many kinds of creatures.

The Christmas village sometimes settles under the Christmas tree, sometimes on the mantel. One year it appeared on the wide window sill of the living-room casement window.

My village always contains the treasures I've collected from other lands—the little wooden figure of the Norwegian girl with a long trumpet calling her herd of goats; the colorful Swedish horses that are now so popular; the horses' cousin, the zebra, made of wood with a grain that looks like stripes; the French rooster; the Russian doll; the Chinese dancer; the three little elves and the little straw lamb from Denmark. And mixed in with these are several creatures I've made.

Buildings for the village are made of Bristol board or construction paper in various colors, with doors and windows of small pieces of colored cellophane tape.

The village can be set up on white cotton batting, and if you'd like a lake in your snowy scene, set a piece of unframed mirror on the cotton.

## VILLAGE CHURCH

The focal point of the village is, of course, the church. This one is made of white Bristol board, trimmed with red and green cellophane tape.

The steeple is made from an 8-inch by 7-inch piece of board, cut according to the diagram. Fold on dotted lines and glue together, tucking in tab to from a four-sided steeple. The points of the steeple are held together with strips of colored cellophane tape—I used green along the points (the roof) and then I covered the corners of the four walls with red tape, to give definition to the little structure. The door is made of one green strip and one red strip of cellophane tape, tapered at the top.

For the main part of the church, start with a piece of board 12 inches long and 3¾ inches wide. Cut according to the diagram, and fold along the dotted

59

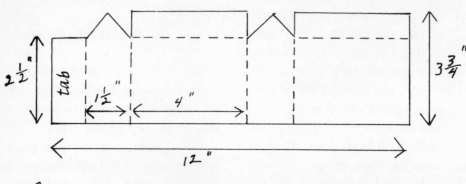

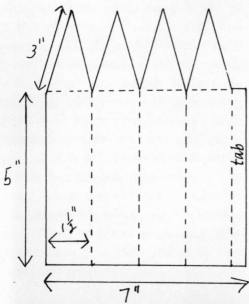

lines. Glue together, tucking tab inside one wall.

The roof is held together with cellophane tape and the corners and eaves are outlined with tape. The windows are small pieces of cellophane tape, pointed to match the door.

You can, if you like, attach the steeple to the church. I leave mine separate because it is easier to store away.

## THE ROOSTER

The rooster is made in bright colors. Use construction paper, Bristol board, or metallic foil. I used construction paper for mine.

### Start with a Circle

Cut a circle 6 inches in diameter. Using only about one third of the circle, staple together to form a cone. Snip off the point of the cone ½ inch down.

Cut out the head, following the pattern given here. Fit the long tab into the cone and fasten with a touch of Sobo glue.

For the rooster's tail, cut two strips, each ½ inch wide: one strip 4 inches long and the other 3½ inches long. Make them of different colors. Fringe the ends, curl them around a pencil, and glue or staple them to the base of the cone so they will stand up as shown in the photograph.

Good colors to use for the rooster: Yellow for the body, red for the head and lower tail, green for the upper tail; blue for the body, yellow for the head and lower tail, red for the upper tail. Whatever colors you use, mix them up and make them bright, for the rooster should be perky.

## VILLAGE BARN

The village barn and silo are made of red construction paper. Let the children make this one—it's simple to put together and the pieces are easy to cut.

For the barn cut a piece of paper 18 inches long and 4 inches wide. Cut according to the diagram, using the measurements given. Fold along the dotted lines indicated in the sketch and glue together, tucking the tab inside one wall. This will give you a barn 6 inches long, 2½ inches wide, and 4 inches high.

For the roof cut a piece of paper 5½ inches by 6½ inches, which will allow for a bit of overhang, and fold on dotted lines as indicated in the diagram. Fasten it to the barn with a few spots of glue.

The silo sits beside the barn—it is not attached to it. Cut a strip 9 inches long and 6 inches wide. Staple the short edges together to form the tower. For the silo roof, cut a 5-inch circle, make a slit from one edge to the center, and then overlap the two resulting edges until you have the desired cone shape— you will use about three quarters of the circle. Staple together and glue to the silo tower.

roof

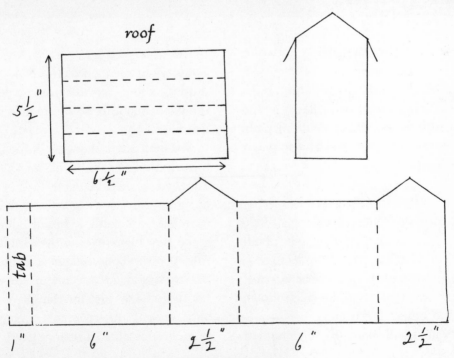

$5\frac{1}{2}"$

$6\frac{1}{2}"$

tab

1"    6"    $2\frac{1}{2}"$    6"    $2\frac{1}{2}"$

63

## THE MOUSE

One of the most ingratiating creatures in my Christmas village is the little white mouse. He is made of plain white paper—regular bond typing paper is excellent.

*Start with a Circle*

Out of plain white paper cut a circle 6 inches in diameter. Using only about one third of the circle, as indicated in the diagram shown here, form a cone, stapling it more than an inch down from the edge of the cone.

With a small pair of scissors, cut away about an inch of the cone on the stapled side (see diagram), tapering the cone smoothly so the mouse will sit down.

A 6-inch strip of paper, ¼ inch wide, is curled up (use a pencil for this) and attached with cellophane tape or a bit of glue for his tail. Attach large rounded ears with a bit of glue, and make tiny black eyes with pen and ink. And presto! Your mouse is completed.

I always make several of these—one for the village, one for the cheese tray, and several to scamper among the branches of the Christmas tree.

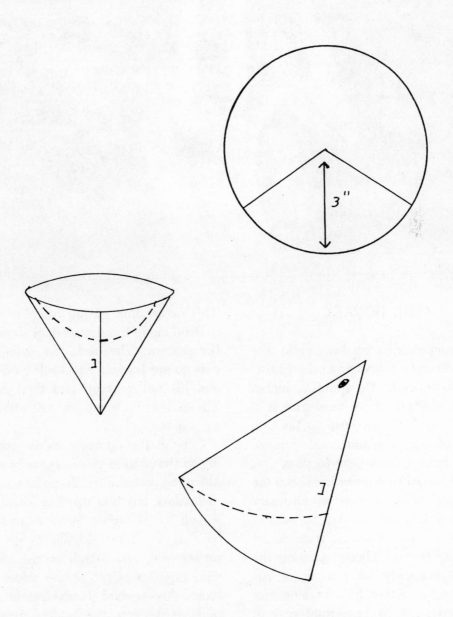

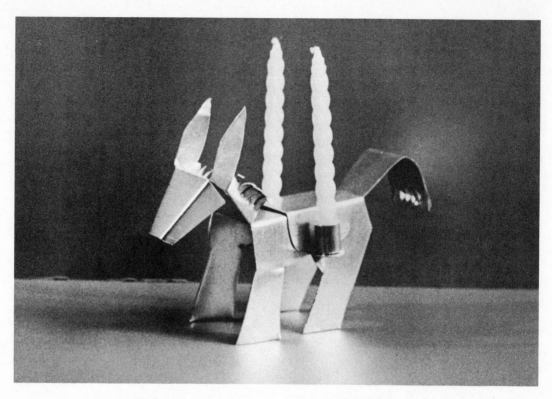

## THE DONKEY

Carrying candles on his saddle, the donkey brings a soft glow to the Christmas village scene. He stands 4 inches high—to the tip of his ears—and is 6 inches long from his nose to his tail. He's made of aluminum, and thus, of course, is kept from year to year.

Trace the pattern given here onto the aluminum with a pencil. Ordinary household scissors will cut the aluminum quite easily—it always reminds me of cutting through cheese. Cutting the donkey accurately takes a bit of patience and care, but he's fetching and he's sturdy, and he lasts from year to year.

Smooth the rough edges with sandpaper or an emery board, and polish very gently with the finest steel wool.

This makes him gleam like pewter.

Bend along the dotted lines shown in the pattern: The neck, the mane, the ears go up; his face and jowls go down; and his tail goes up and then down. The curls in his mane and tail will form as you cut.

Cut out the donkey's saddle according to the pattern given, again bending along the dotted lines. To make the candleholders, cut two strips of aluminum ½ inch by 1⅝ inches. Bend around the base of a 3½-inch candle to get the proper size, and attach to the saddle with liquid solder. Let the solder dry thoroughly—several hours—before putting candles into the holders. Use the non-drip kind.

Paint the saddle a bright color, or polish it with steel wool for a silvery shine.

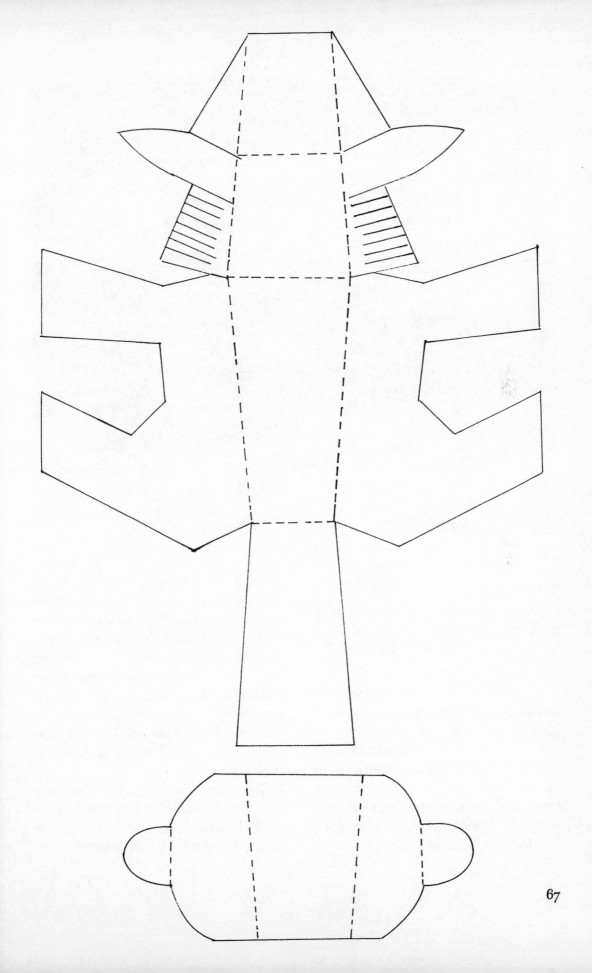

67

## THE FIRESIDE CAT

The fireside cat and her kitten can be made of construction paper (which I used), metallic foil, or Bristol board.

*Start with a Circle*

For the cat, cut a circle 10 inches in diameter; and for the kitten, use a circle 5 inches in diameter.

Form a cone of about one third of the circle, and staple it together. Snip off the point of the cone (about ⅛ inch), and make two tiny slits, one opposite the other, at the top of the cone for the cat's head to fit into.

A circle 2 inches in diameter makes the big cat's head; the kitten's is 1 inch in diameter. Slip the head into the slits and secure with a drop of Sobo glue.

Make ears 1½ inches long for the cat, 1 inch long for the kitten. Make them pointed and crease them through the center, folding them slightly toward the face. Make whiskers of sprigs of evergreen or of paper, and attach with Sobo glue.

The tail of the cat is 6 inches long and ½ inch wide. Curl it over a pencil and attach with glue or cellophane tape. The kitten's tail is 4 inches long.

## THE THREE WISE MEN

The Three Wise Men, in their royal garb, are a part of every Christmas scene. Make them of colorful paper or foil, and choose your colors with care. My kings are blue and purple and red—all royal colors. The blue one has a crown and cope of green; the purple one has a pink crown and cope; and the red one has gold.

### Start with a Circle

Make a cone of one quarter of a 9-inch circle—this will give you a slender cone. Cut the cope according to the pattern given. Fasten it around the shoulders of the king with a spot of glue, overlapping the points until they form a smooth, curved line for the cope from front to back.

Cut the crown from the pattern given (same color for the crown and cope) and form a ring by overlapping the two points and securing with glue. Slip the crown over the point of the cone. Fasten with a dab of glue.

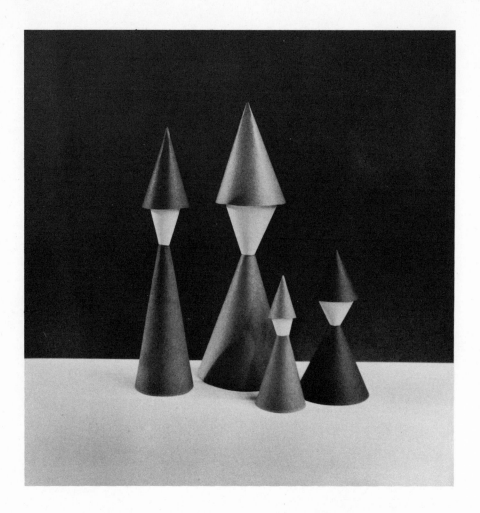

## THE *TOMTE*

In Scandinavia the Christmas elf is called a *tomte* (tom'-tah). *Tomtes* are almost always red and are made of paper, wood, yarn, foil, and even of straw, and are used to decorate everything from Christmas trees to packages. And usually there are *tomtes* on the Christmas dinner table.

Here is a modern version of the Christmas *tomte*. These are made of construction paper—red for the body and cap, and white for the head—and they can be tall or short, fat or slim.

### Start with a Circle

The tall *tomte* in the center of the photograph is about 10 inches high. Cut a circle of red construction paper 10 inches in diameter. Using only about one third of the circle, form a cone and staple or glue it together. Snip off about ½ inch of the point of the cone.

Next, cut a circle of white construction paper 5½ inches in diameter. Again

using only one third of the circle, form a cone and fasten it with staples or glue.

Dip a toothpick into Sobo glue, run it around the inside of the "neck" of the red cone, and insert the pointed end of the white cone, thus fastening the head to the body.

The third cone—which will be the cap—is made of a circle 7 inches in diameter, cut from red construction paper. Once more, using only one third of the circle, form a cone and fasten it together with glue or staples.

Again dip the toothpick in the glue,

and this time run it around the outside edge of the top of the white cone, and set the cap on the head. In a few moments the glue will dry—and your *tomte* will be finished.

For a slimmer elf, use less than a third of the circle for each of the three cones. And if you'd like him to be fatter, use about half of the circle. This, of course, will also make him shorter.

These little creatures add color and charm to the Christmas Eve buffet, the mantel, or along the stairway as shown here.

CHAPTER V

# DECORATIONS THAT HANG

Paper and foil are the most popular materials for making decorations that hang. All the shades and hues of the rainbow are available in these materials—and color is half the fun of making decorations. Make the same decoration in, say, red and blue, and then make it in yellow and green, and the one will appear to be quite different from the other.

Circles and squares, stars and strips—all the geometric shapes are used. And they should be cut as accurately as possible to give the decoration a proper finish, a perfect balance, and a pleasing proportion.

To cut a circle use a compass to draw a pattern—if you have a compass. If you do not have a compass, tie a string to the point of a pencil and use as you would a compass. Hold the string with one finger at the center point and draw your circle just as you would with a compass.

Simpler than that is to find a saucer, a bowl, or a cup of about the size you want, and trace around it. You can also cut a circle from a square by folding the square in half and then in half

again, and then making a curved cut from one corner to the corner opposite it, eliminating the point that has no folded edges. Fold as shown in the sketch and cut along the broken line.

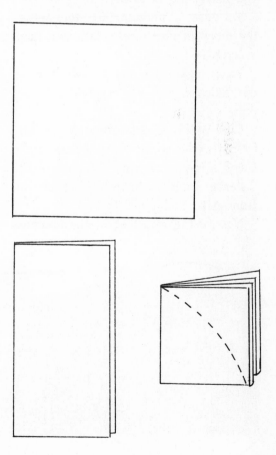

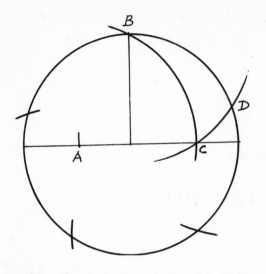

The easiest way to cut a star shape is to follow a pattern. But sometimes the pattern you have will not give you a star of the size you want; in that case you must make a pattern for your star.

To draw a five-pointed star, follow the diagram given here. You will need a compass.

First, make the circle and draw in the diameter and the perpendicular radius.

Find point A, the center of the line from the edge to the center of the circle. Using a radius on your compass of the distance from A to B, swing an arc from A to find point C.

Next, using a radius on the compass of the distance from B to C, swing an arc from B to find point D.

The distance from B to D is a fifth of the circle—use this measurement to find the five equally distant points around the circle.

Draw lines between the points, and you'll have your star.

A six-pointed star is simpler to make. Cut a circle of paper. Fold it in half and then fold in thirds, and then fold in half again. Cut along dotted line as shown in the diagram. Open it up and you have a six-pointed star.

Many of the decorations that follow can be folded up and packed away for the next season.

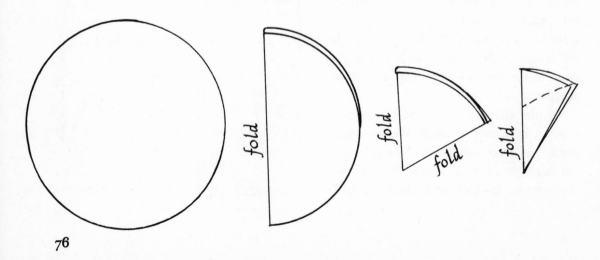

## PUFF BALL

Puff balls in white or in vibrant colors will trim your tree with distinction.

*Start with a Circle*

Cut twelve 3-inch circles of the paper and color of your choice (you can use tissue paper, gold wrapping paper, shelf paper, or plain white bond, and use twice as many circles if you choose tissue paper).

Without making any crease except just at the point, fold each circle in half and then in half again. The whole secret of making the puff ball is to make segments without creases.

Using strong thread—preferably nylon —sew through the corner of each segment, as shown in the diagram. Secure the knot by sewing twice through the first segment. If you are making your puff ball of tissue paper, sew through a

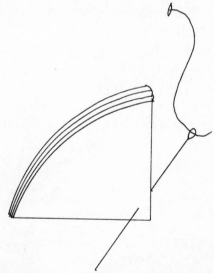

tiny circle of cardboard before stringing the segments on the thread, and then finish with another tiny piece. Otherwise, the thread may tear the delicate paper.

Pull thread up tight to form a ball. Fasten securely by sewing once more through the last segment, and suspend the ball by the same thread.

## SWEDISH TISSUE-PAPER BALL

The Swedish tissue-paper ball is effective on a Christmas tree, or suspended in a doorway, where it will twirl with the air currents.

### Start with a Circle

Cut twenty-five circles (cut several at a time) about 5 inches in diameter. Divide each circle into six equal parts (fold in half and then into thirds, and make strong creases), and cut to within an inch of the center. (See next page.)

Roll each segment from one side to the other over a ⅜-inch dowel or a slim pencil (sometimes I use a nut pick!). Twist the tip, and slip out the dowel. It is simple to do, but time-consuming, as you can see, and it does require a bit of patience.

Each circle will give you six spikes, and no glue is necessary. When the segments of all twenty-five circles are rolled up, sew through the center of each circle, starting and ending with a tiny circle of cardboard so as not to tear the fragile tissue paper. Pull thread up tight to form a round ball, and fasten thread. Suspend by the same thread.

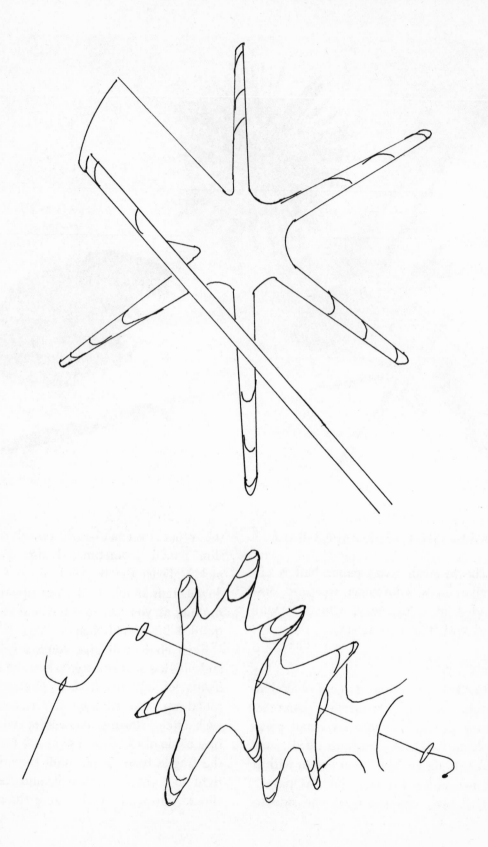

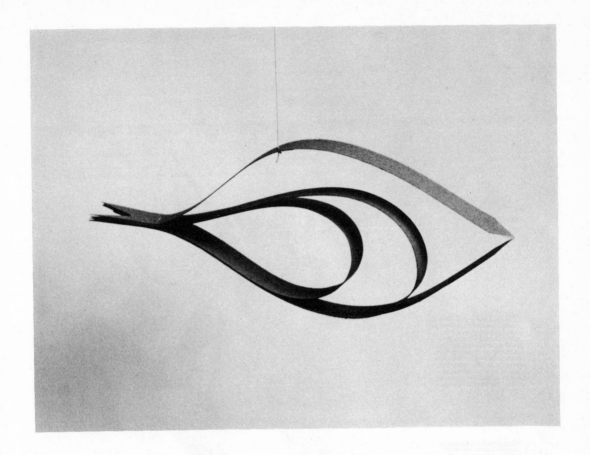

## FISH

Paper of some rigidity, such as construction paper, works very well for the fish. I usually make mine in two colors.

### Start with a Strip

The fish takes three strips, each ¾ inch wide: one 17 inches long, one 14 inches long, and one 11 inches long. This will give you a fish 8 inches long.

Fold the longest strip in half and crease the fold. Bend the other two strips in half but do not crease, thus forming loops. Place the shortest strip—looped—inside the next—also looped. Place the longest strip on the outside. Make sure all the ends are evenly matched (all six of them) and staple them together about 1½ inches from the end. Notch the tail (the stapled end) and make a point for the nose, without cutting off so much that the fish will be cut in two.

Suspend by a thread, experimenting to find out just where the thread should be so that your fish will be properly balanced. The fish should swim horizontally, and since the tail is heavier than the nose, the thread should be slightly off-center, toward the tail.

Make a mobile of three, five, or seven fish, using fish that are about half as large, but made in the same proportion. For instructions, see the chapter on mobiles.

## HEART TWIRLER

Red is the obvious color for the heart, but it is effective in other colors too. Use construction paper or metallic foil.

### Start with a Strip

First, cut seven strips, each about ½ inch wide, in these lengths: two strips 9 inches; two 7½ inches; two 6 inches; and one (for the center) 4 inches. This gives you three pairs and a single one for the stem.

Second, arrange the strips for sta-pling: Hold the 4-inch strip (which goes down through the center of the heart) downward. All the others are held upward and are graduated on either side of the center strip—the longest ones are placed on either side of the center strip, then the next size, and finally the 6-inch size on the outside. Staple through all seven strips, as shown in the photograph.

Third, pull all the strips down, three on each side of the center stem, making sure the ends are all even with the bottom of the center strip. Staple securely. Suspend by a thread.

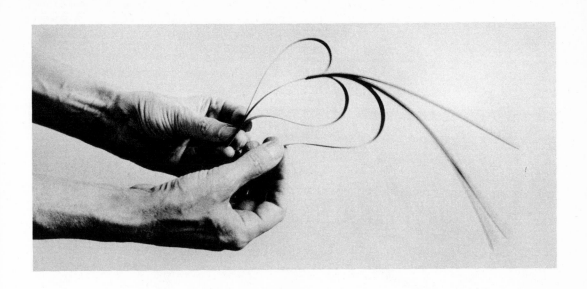

## SINGLE TWIRLER

I used two colors for my single twirler—Chinese red and moss green. But you can make it all of a shade, gold and silver, green and blue, or choose a different color for each strip. Some rigidity is needed to make the strips bow properly. Use metallic foil, colored construction paper, or Bristol board.

## THE THREE RINGS

Loops within loops, and each in a different color, can be suspended in a doorway or on a Christmas tree. Metallic foil or construction paper is good for this one.

*Start with a Strip*

Cut three strips ¾ inch wide, each one in a different color, in these lengths: 18 inches, 15 inches, and 12 inches.

With the shortest strip on top, then the next, and finally the longest, match all the ends, lap them over about ½ inch, staple them together. Suspend by a black thread.

*Start with a Strip*

All seven strips are the same width: ¾ inch. The center one measures 5½ inches long, the next two (one on each side of the center one) are 6 inches long; and the outside strips are 7 inches long.

Match ends, top and bottom, staple them together, and suspend by a thread.

## DOUBLE TWIRLER

Double twirlers are excellent breeze-catchers. I used blue, red, and yellow for mine, which gives the decoration a sort of country-cousin look. It's reminiscent of the designs one finds on furniture in the Pennsylvania Dutch countryside and in the mountains of Norway.

*Start with a Strip*

The center strip is 8½ inches long.

The next two are 10 inches long; the next two are 11½ inches long; and the outside strips are 13 inches long. All are ¾ inch wide.

Make sure the two matching strips (the two outer ones, the next two, etc.) are exactly the same length, so the twirler will not be lopsided.

Staple ends together, top and bottom, making sure they all meet exactly.

Then staple all strips together just below the mid-point of the center stem, making the double bow. Suspend by a thread.

## SEGMENTED CHRISTMAS BALL

Red or green construction paper, gold or silver metallic foil are ideal for the segmented Christmas ball.

### Start with a Circle

Out of the paper of your choice cut nine circles 4 inches in diameter. Fold each circle in half and crease them through the center. Open them up, stack them together, and on the crease staple them together at top, at bottom, and in the middle.

Alternating top and bottom, fasten together with a small dab of glue the outer edges of the segments about a third of the way down (and up). Run a thread through the center top of all nine circles—and hang it up.

[14] The little church nestles into the hillside surrounded by *tomtes* and an angel. See Chapter IV.

[15] The village church is made in two sections. Patterns and instructions are given in Chapter IV.

[16] Christmas *tomtes* (sprites) admire the glitter tree. They are made of paper cones. For details see Chapter IV.

[17] The wise men arrive at the village barn. Instructions for making these figures and the barn are given in Chapter IV.

[18] The Christmas cross from Sweden, hand-carved from a single piece of wood, stands beside a group of gold-foil angels. See Chapter VII.

[19] Tree of Christmas balls makes the buffet centerpiece or trims the hallway table. For instructions see Chapter II.

[20] A candle-topped tree with three little angels brightens the hall table. Tree is described in Chapter II.

[21] The harlequin angel accents the greenery along a balcony railing. Details are given in Chapter VII. Instructions for making the mouse are in Chapter IV.

[23] A centerpiece of apples, big and small, holds nine candles and is decorated with sprigs of evergreen. See Chapter II.

[22] The wise men are greeted by the donkey and *tomtes*, along the ledge of a stairway. See Chapter IV.

[24] Place cards that stand upright made from Christmas-card cutouts dress up the party table. For instructions see Chapter IX.

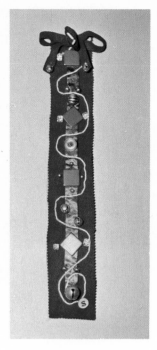

[25] A treasure *klockasträng* for the door is made of trinkets and treasures, bells and gold braid. See Chapter I.

[26] A crèche for the mantel or under the Christmas tree has figures of Christmas-card cutouts. See Chapter IX.

[27] Christmas jewelry made of aluminum can be decorated with glitter and various colors. Instructions are given in Chapter X.

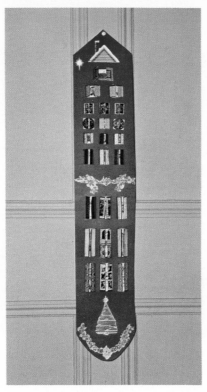

[28] An Advent calendar in the form of a *klockasträng* is made with last year's Christmas cards. See Chapter IX.

[29] A ring of copper angels holding candles is suspended over the copper coffeepot. See Chapter III.

[30] Orange-juice cans painted gold and tied with red bows and evergreen boughs give glamour to the kitchen door. See Chapter I.

[31] Strips of felt cut with pinking scissors and trimmed with sleigh bells and gold cowbell make traditional *klockasträng*. See Chapter I.

[32] A pink tissue-paper tree combines with little white figures. See Chapter II for instructions for making the tree.

[34] The frosty look of the snowball tree makes a wintry scene. For complete details see Chapter II.

[33] Colors of the door swag and doorknob decoration should blend well. Instructions for both are given in Chapter I.

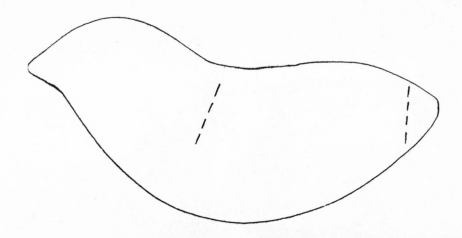

## SWEDISH CHRISTMAS BIRD

The Swedish Christmas bird is traditionally suspended over the Christmas dinner table, bringing good luck to the household.

Follow the pattern given here. It was sent to me from Sweden many years ago. The body of the bird is made of Bristol board or cardboard. The wings and tail are tissue paper. Cut two strips, each 5 inches wide and 9 inches long. Fold and snip the strips exactly as with the snowflake that is in this chapter.

Make two slits in the body, as indicated by the broken lines in the pattern. With manicure scissors (or embroidery scissors), widen each slit to about 1/16 inch so that the wings and tail can be slipped through.

Secure both sides of the wings and tail to the body with small pieces of cellophane tape. Spread out the wings. Fasten the center of the tail together with cellophane tape so that it forms a semicircle. Suspend the bird by a

thread run through the body at a point off-center toward the back, making sure the bird is properly balanced. You may have to experiment to find the balance point.

The birds are made in all colors and in white.

## PAPER ANGEL

An angel of paper to hang in a doorway—simple to make. She really floats, whether she is made of gold foil or colored construction paper.

Cut one body and two wings, using the patterns given here. Choose one color for the angel body and another for the wings. My angel is blue and she has chartreuse wings.

Staple or glue wings to body, with the points of the wings facing toward the head and one wing slightly forward of the other. Bend wings out from the body a little so that the angel becomes three-dimensional. Run a thread through the body—experimenting until you find the right spot so she will balance—and hang her up. If you want to keep her for another year, fold the wings together and place her in the bottom of the Christmas box.

Three angels, each of a different color or all of gold or silver, can be attached to wires to make a mobile. For instructions, see the chapter on mobiles.

## TRADITIONAL BIRD

One of the nicest symbols of the Christmas season is the bird—a reminder of the new year to come. Here's a simple one to make.

Cut out one body and two wings, using the pattern given here. Make your bird of construction paper or metallic foil, with the body of one color and the wings of another. Staple the wings to the body (or use glue) and bend wings slightly away from the body. Suspend by a thread run through the body. Make sure your bird will balance—if the thread is too far back, his head will drop!

Three, five, or seven birds can be used for a mobile. For instructions, see the chapter on mobiles.

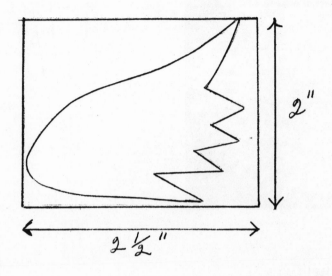

2"

2 1/2 "

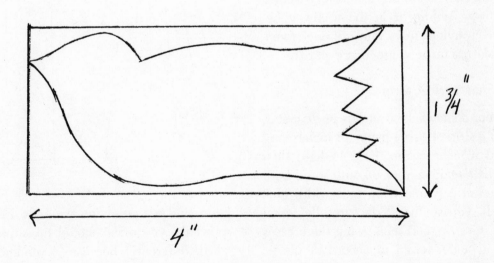

1 3/4 "

4 "

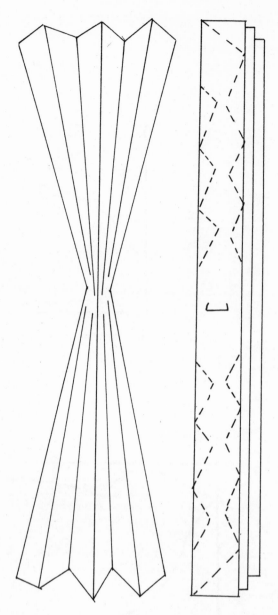

## SNOWFLAKE

Snowflakes are particularly appealing when they are hung in clusters from a hallway ceiling or in the archway between living room and dining room. Make them of white tissue paper.

### Start with a Strip

For a snowflake 6 inches in diameter, cut a strip of tissue paper 18 inches long and 6 inches wide. Fold in half, then in half again, and again, and so on until your strip is folded up to a width of ½ inch. Crease the folds carefully, open up the strip, and then, using the creases as a guide, refold in accordion pleats.

When the strip is again folded up to a width of ½ inch, staple in the middle, across the width (see sketch). Snip out tiny triangular pieces on each side of the folded strip, as shown in the diagram, and cut points on the ends. Each snowflake you make should be snipped a little differently, because, as you know, snowflakes are never alike.

Open up to form a circle and fasten the sides together with cellophane tape. Suspend by a thread slipped through one of the triangular cutouts.

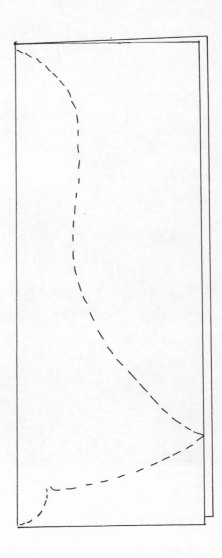

## SEGMENTED PAPER BELL

Many kinds of paper and foil are good to use for the paper bell. Plain white bond is especially effective.

*Start with a Rectangle*

Out of fifteen rectangles 4½ inches by 5 inches, cut fifteen bells, following the pattern given. Fold each bell in half and make a strong crease. Flatten out the bells, stack them up, and staple three times along the crease, at top, at bottom, and in the middle. Gently fold each segment away from the next until the bell is completely opened up. Run a thread through the top of the bell, and hang it up.

## SIX-POINTED PAPER STAR

First cut a pattern for a six-pointed star, following directions given at the beginning of this chapter.

### Start with a Square

Out of fifteen squares, cut fifteen stars, and make your decoration just as the bell is made.

You can go right on, making all kinds of shapes in this fashion—a five-pointed star, a heart, a snowball. Make up your own patterns or follow some of those given here. Be sure your design is symmetrical so it will hang properly, and fill your tree with paper balls, all of a color or all colors of the rainbow. I like to make them of plain white bond paper (regular typing paper). They look crisp and snowy.

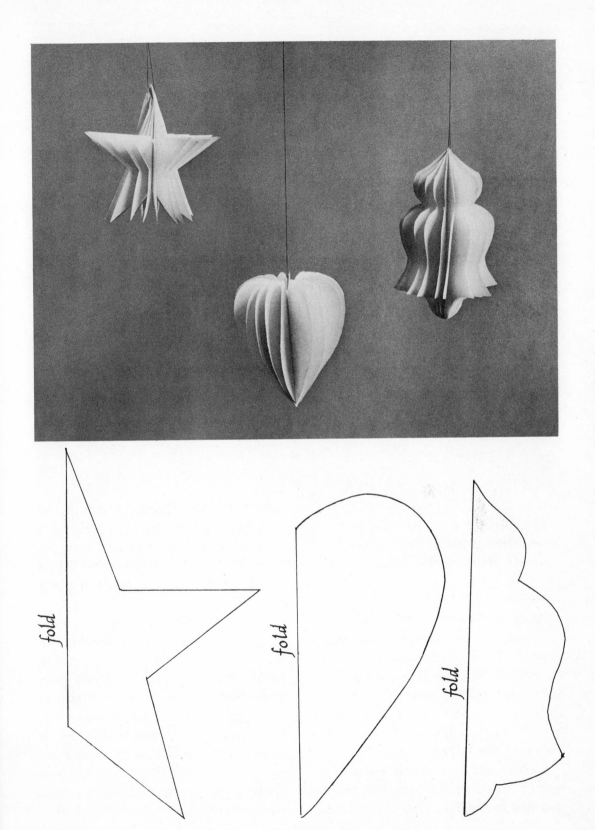

## SPIRAL BREEZE-CATCHER

The spiral breeze-catcher is made of construction paper or Bristol board, in whatever color you like.

### Start with a Circle

Using a compass, draw a circle 6 inches in diameter. Within this circle, draw circles ½ inch apart, until you have six circles in all, as in the diagram. With a pencil and ruler, very lightly divide in quarters, as shown. These quarter lines will be guidelines in sketching the spirals.

Each of the four spirals starts at a quarter mark. Sketch carefully before you start to cut. Your spiral lines should progress inward ½ inch per quarter, all the way into the center (see dotted lines in diagram). You can erase on both construction paper and Bristol board, so if your curves do not suit you, try again!

Cut around outside circle. Then cut along dotted lines, using manicure scissors, until you have four separate spirals. Suspend a paper ball (see page 77 for instructions on how to make it) or a small Christmas ball in the center, and hang the breeze-catcher by a thread. Place it where there are air currents and it will spin slowly and constantly, and you'll find it's an eye-catcher as well as a breeze-catcher!

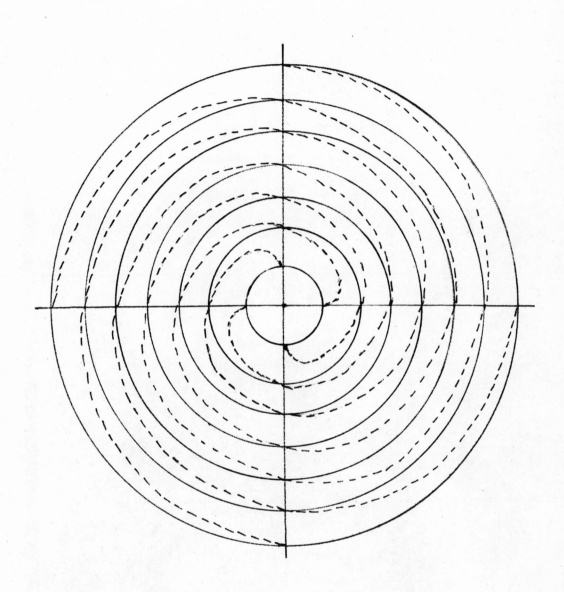

☆

# CHAPTER VI

# ACCENT YOUR TREASURES

Some of our treasures are heirlooms, beautiful in themselves but treasured too because they came from Great-grandfather's house. Some of our treasures we choose ourselves—a bowl, a plate, a candlestick, perhaps from a foreign land.

When the holiday season arrives and packages pile up, the Christmas tree takes over the house, and bells and bows abound. When the wreaths are all in place and your decorations seem to be complete, give your décor distinction—accent a treasure or two.

If the antique table in the hall has had its beauty buried by boxes, papers, and tags, bring it back into the picture—give it a holiday bouquet.

If the old pewter has been relegated to the top shelf of the china cabinet, polish it up and make it the focal point of the mantel, with a spray of holly and a grouping of candles.

If the tray you bought last summer on your trip to Mexico has been stacked away in the pantry, take it out and fill it with cookies for friends and family alike.

Our treasues can turn our holidays into a party season. And the simplest touch will do the trick—try it and see!

## THE WOODEN MORTAR

A choice and cherished treasure, such as this wooden mortar from Great-grandmother's day, adds to the beauty of an arrangement of dried foliage, seed pods, and berries.

The orange-red of the berries is repeated in the Scandinavian tapestry under the mortar, giving the setting a Christmas atmosphere.

The mortar does double duty at Christmas time. Before it gets its holiday bouquet it goes to work, along with its pestle, to grind up the cardamom seed that gives the Christmas raisin bread (*julekake*) and the Christmas cakes (*bakkels*) their distinctive flavor. Cardamom can be found in some shops already ground, but if you grind your own you'll find the pungent aroma and the flavor of freshly ground cardamom seeds are beyond compare.

## PEWTER AND HOLLY

The patina of old pewter is picked up by the silvery-gray branches of the high-bush blueberry. Sprigs of holly are fastened to one side of the plate with floral clay, forming a sort of tiny "pool" for the bird perched in the holly. Two more birds in the branches, unaware of Great-grandmother's pitcher and oil lamp, seem to be waiting for their chance to fly to the holly.

Interesting shadows can be created by the proper placing of a lamp on a nearby table.

## MIDNIGHT
## ON NEW YEAR'S EVE

Take Grandmother's doll and Grandfather's clock down off the shelf for the holidays. Together they will remind you of the magic hour of New Year's Eve.

A tiny arrangement of evergreens gives a seasonal touch to the treasures.

## A CANDLE BY THE SOFA

Here's a tiny touch of Christmas for the table by the sofa.

A liqueur glass, slender and only 5 inches tall, is inverted over tiny sprigs of evergreen—use juniper or princess pine or cryptomeria.

Attach a 3-inch candle to the bottom (which has now become the top) of the glass with a drop of melted wax or with floral clay, and add a few sprigs of evergreen around the base of the candle to conceal the wax or clay.

A bit of whimsy to be sure—but it's simple and it's charming, and it has a purpose too. A 3-inch candle, if it is the nondrip variety, will burn for twenty minutes, long enough to contribute a glow to a brief conversation and light your cigarette as well.

## TREASURES UNDER GLASS

Many of us collect tiny creatures and figures on our travels, and often these treasures enhance the Christmas scene. If they are too tiny for the Christmas village—or if you are not planning a village—put them under glass. Turn a wineglass over them, or a liqueur glass or a goblet, depending on the size of the figurine. Fasten a candle to the glass with wax or floral clay, and trim with evergreen. A grouping of such glasses, all with treasures underneath and candles on top, can be an effective centerpiece for the dining table or decoration for the mantel. Mix up the sizes so that the candles are not all the same height.

## THE OLD WELSH DRESSER

The glow of candlelight enhances the china and pewter on the old Welsh dresser.

A simple arrangement of long-needled pine, yew, and dried leaves fills the pewter bowl. Oasis, soaked in water placed in a container inside the bowl, keeps the arrangement fresh throughout the holidays. Sprigs of yew decorate the candles.

## THE CORNER CUPBOARD

The sugar bowl of the pewter coffee set becomes a container for a small bouquet of evergreens and red berries, giving Christmas color to the old-fashioned china in the old-fashioned corner cupboard. A small glass bowl inside the pewter sugar bowl holds a piece of Oasis, which keeps the arrangement fresh.

For more color in the cabinet at Christmas time, pack away a few of the antique pieces and replace them with brightly painted floral plates and a teapot. These not only complement the evergreen bouquet, they stand ready for action for afternoon tea.

## THE SWEDISH PLATE

Coppery-red and grayish-blue are the colors that predominate on the hand-painted Swedish *rosmåling* plate. Here it is resting from its usual chore of carrying crackers to the cocktail table, and is accented by the small bouquet of holly and juniper in a copper Swedish bowl.

## THE BRASS TRAY TABLE
## HOLDS THE TREE

Your favorite folding tray table spends most of the year folded away, to be taken out for an occasional tea party. If the tray is brass, as this one is, put your table-sized Christmas tree on it and fill the tree with Christmas lights. The tray will double the glow by reflecting the lights on its shiny surface.

Along the window sill behind the tree, goblets are turned upside down over Christmas balls to hold a row of red candles.

☆

CHAPTER VII

# SPECIAL FEATURES

Included in this section are decorations that can dominate the décor, the features that might become highlights of your Christmas trimmings.

Sometimes one feature is all we want, and if we find just the right wreath for the window, or exactly the star for the stairway, our trimmings are complete. Here are a few suggestions.

## THE SNOWMAN

This snowman sits by the fireside and never melts away. He has become a "tradition" with the children in my family, and each year he is refurbished with a fresh layer of snowy cotton.

A ten-pound flour bag is the foundation for the body, a five-pound bag for the head.

Place a ¼-inch dowel 15 inches long in the center of the larger bag and stuff crumpled newspapers around it until the bag is filled. Fill the smaller bag with crumpled newspapers and turn it upside down over the top of the dowel, making sure the bag goes down over the top of the ten-pound bag. Tie string tightly around the two bags where they meet, to make the neck.

Cut off the hook of a wire coat hanger, open up the hanger, and stick it right through bag and newspapers (the larger bag) to form the arms. Turn back wire from each end toward the body, so that the arms are formed of double wire. Tie newspapers (folded) around wire, to give shape to the arms.

Cover the bags and the arms with a thin coating of Sobo glue (a paint brush dipped in the glue works very well) and put a layer of cotton batting over the entire snowman. A second layer is placed over the first—it will stick without any more glue—and more layers are added until the snowman is built up to the size you want. Mine is 18 inches tall without his hat. (Page 118.)

Cut eyes and mouth out of black construction paper and glue in place. Glue on a tiny red Christmas ball for the nose. A wide red satin ribbon makes his scarf.

The snowman's hat is made of black construction paper. Cut an oval shape, roughly 5½ inches by 8 inches, and a strip 6½ inches by 12 inches. Staple the strip (the stovepipe) together and glue it to the oval (the brim). Tie a red metallic-foil bell in one hand. This snowman has a red wooden Swedish bird perched beside his hat.

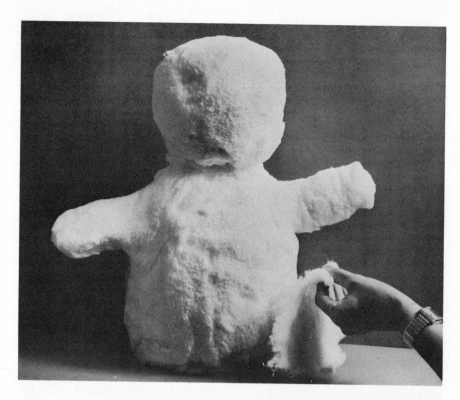

COURTESY OF FLOWER GROWER, PHOTOGRAPH BY KARI BERGGRAV

## A WREATH
## AROUND YOUR WINDOW

Last Christmas instead of putting a wreath in the window, I put the window in a wreath. It turned out to be the hit of our holiday decorations.

I started with eight large branches of long-needled pine and a spool of 22-gauge wire. First, I placed several layers of newspapers on the kitchen floor, roughly drawing with a soft pencil a circle about 60 inches in diameter—my window is a little less than 60 inches square. The newspaper pattern served only as a guide.

Then, following the natural curve of the branches, I wired them together, hiding the wire in the needles at each turn and making the curve of the branches conform to the penciled circle

119

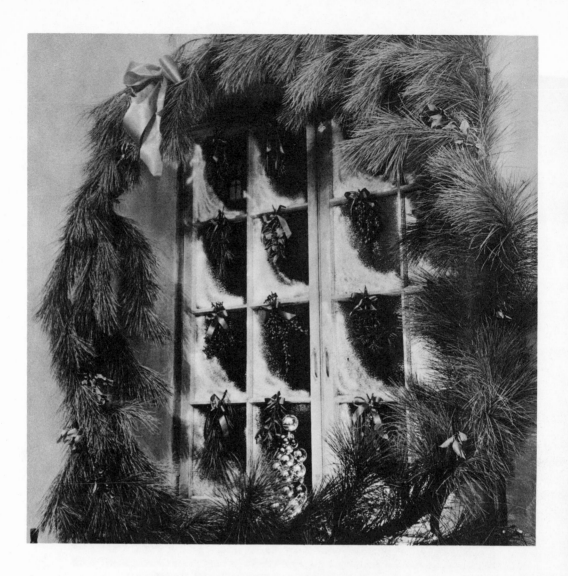

on the newspapers. I wound the wire continuously, not breaking it once, until the entire wreath was finished.

Wear work gloves if you use long-needled pine, as the branches are covered with pitch.

When the wreath was finished, it was suspended from the ceiling molding by picture hooks and wire.

In each of the sixteen small panes in the window I hung a sprig of evergreen, each a different kind and each tied with red ribbon. And I sprayed the panes with artificial snow to make it a wintry window.

The evergreens I used were juniper, holly, boxwood, balsam, bayberry, mistletoe, cryptomeria, yew, spruce, hemlock, long-needled pine, azalea, rhododendron, mountain laurel, and two kinds of heather.

A red satin bow on the wreath and a Christmas-ball tree on the window sill completed the picture.

## THE MIDAS TOUCH

Many of us like to make bouquets and arrangements of dried plant material that has been sprayed with gold paint. One of my friends goes all the way and sprays the container too.

This golden container for the golden bouquet is made of a soft-drink bottle. The bouquet consists of dried hibiscus seed pods and one dried hibiscus blossom (dried in silica gel) sprayed with gold. Circled with sprigs of yew, the arrangement gives a Midas touch to a hall table.

## TWELVE-POINTED STAR

The twelve-pointed star is easy to make from gold or silver gift-wrapping paper or from metallic foil of any color. Add it to evergreen branches on your door, use it to accent a stairway festoon, or tie it with ribbons for each side of your mantel and illuminate it with a candle.

Cut two circles, one 6 inches and one 5½ inches in diameter. Divide each circle into six equal parts, as you would a pie, and cut each segment to within an inch of the center of the circle. Cut a ½-inch hole in the center of each circle. (See page 124.)

Then form points of each segment by folding back and stapling together (do not crease) the corners of the segment. You will now have two stars, each with six points.

For the center of the star use a colored Christmas ball, or use cranberries as I did. Attach an 8-inch wire (22-gauge) to each of seven cranberries (or to a 1-inch Christmas ball) and

COURTESY OF FLOWER GROWER,
PHOTOGRAPH BY JOHN R. WHITING

twist the wires together. Draw wires through the center hole of the smaller circle and then through the larger circle and through a 1½-inch block of Styrofoam, twisting wire back upon itself to secure. Arrange the points of the star so that they alternate, giving you a twelve-pointed star.

Evergreens may be inserted into the Styrofoam backing block.

## THE CONE ANGEL

Golden angels made of cones can be used in many ways. Here they stand, three together, decorated with cryptomeria.

### Start with a Circle

Gold Christmas wrapping paper is good for these. Make the diameter of your circle twice as long as the height you'd like your angel to be. For instance, for an angel 5 inches tall, cut a circle 10 inches in diameter—which is the size of the circle I used for the tallest one shown in the photograph. The medium-sized angel is 3½ inches tall (a 7-inch circle) and the littlest angel is 2¼ inches tall (a 4½-inch circle). Make a cut from the edge of the circle to the center, overlapping the cut edges to form a cone. Secure with dabs of glue. This way of making a cone (instead of cutting off a third of the circle) gives extra sturdiness to a lightweight paper. It works well with the gold wrapping paper.

Follow the patterns given for the wings. Before you cut, fold the gold paper double, so the wrong sides are on the inside. Cut out the wings and with a toothpick put a few very tiny spots of glue between the two pieces of paper.

Snip off the point of the cone and fasten with glue a silver Christmas ball of about the right size for the head. Attach wings with glue. Make a halo of a piece of gold cord, and glue the halo just above the wings.

If this is the year of the angel, make them of cones—and make them gold!

## HARLEQUIN ANGEL

An angel without wings is the harlequin angel, and she comes from Scandinavia.

### Start with a Circle

Use red construction paper or gold Christmas wrapping paper. Cut a circle 5 inches in diameter.

Fold the circle in half, and again in half, and again and again, until the circle is folded into pie-shaped sections that measure 1 inch at the outer edge and taper to a point at the center.

Unfold, and then refold in accordion pleats, using the first fold marks as a guide.

Cut a circle 1¾ inches in diameter of white construction paper (or silver wrapping paper if you are using gold wrapping for the body). Through the center of the white circle and down through the center of the pleated red circle, insert the stem of a small silver Christmas ball—the kind that has a pipe-cleaner stem.

For the hat, cut a circle of red (or gold) 3½ inches in diameter. Using only about a quarter of the circle, form a cone that will fit the Christmas-ball head. Staple it together and attach to the head with a few dabs of glue.

Let the harlequin sit among your greens or place her on plate glass to get the full benefit of her reflected glory.

## THE DOUBLE ANGEL RING

Hang an angel ring in the hallway or over the buffet table. The double angel ring has six cone angels in two sizes— the larger ones 2¼ inches tall and the smaller ones, on the top, 1¾ inches tall.

Two wooden embroidery hoops are used, an 8-inch and a 6-inch. Cut three pieces of gold cord 15 inches long, and tie them to the hoops, placing the upper hoop about 4½ inches above the lower one.

Attach the angels to the hoops, between the cords, by gluing the back of the skirts to the hoops. This makes the angels stand away from the hoop. Wind princess pine around the hoops (this will give the angels something to stand on!) and secure the pine with very fine wire. Knot the three strands of gold cord together and hang the angel ring from a wall bracket or from the ceiling.

## SINGLE ANGEL RING

The angels on the single ring are made of brightly colored foil. Their double wings (see pattern) give them a three-dimensional look. Fold the front wings slightly forward.

Cut the angel bodies according to the pattern given. Cover the halo and feet with a thin coating of Sobo glue and sprinkle with gold or silver glitter. Then glue on the wings—first the smaller ones and then the larger.

Tie three pieces of gold cord, each 15 inches long, to a 6-inch embroidery hoop at evenly spaced intervals, and fasten them in place with glue.

In between the cords, glue the angels to the hoop. Wind princess pine or cryptomeria around the hoop and use very fine wire to hold the pine in place.

Knot the ends of the three pieces of cord together—make sure the angel ring hangs level—and suspend from a wall bracket.

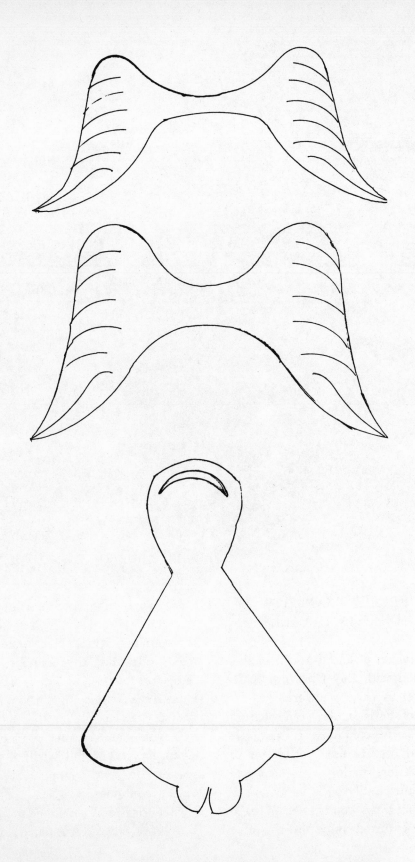

## BLUEBERRY BRANCHES
## AND CHRISTMAS BALLS

Two branches of high-bush blueberry are trimmed with tiny Christmas balls to make an asymmetrical "tree."

Plaster of Paris is ideal for securing branches in the container. It is simple to mix and easy to use. Add water to the dry plaster, stirring with a spatula or wide knife, until you have a smooth mixture about the consistency of cake frosting. (I mixed mine in a coffee can.) Pour into container and insert branches. The plaster will set in about ten minutes, which gives you time to make sure that the branches are arranged as you would like to have them. Hold them in place until the plaster begins to set.

If you want to use your container again, line it with foil before filling with plaster. By gently tapping the bottom of the container, you can remove the plaster—provided the container has straight or tapered sides, as shown here.

## HEARTS ON THE
## BLUEBERRY BRANCH

In Scandinavia the heart is a favorite design at Christmas time. This "tree" is made of a single branch of high-bush blueberry trimmed with 1½-inch red hearts from Sweden, made of very thin wood.

The branch is set in plaster of Paris in a coffee can painted with red enamel and trimmed with gold braid secured with glue.

The hearts can be made of heavy red paper, metallic foil, or balsa wood painted red. And the tree could be used for Christmas or for St. Valentine's Day.

Other branches, of course, can be used, but the blueberry is particularly interesting because of its gnarled and windswept form and its silvery-gray sheen.

## CHRISTMAS TREE FOR THE BIRDS

"The birds shall have their Christmas tree before we have our own." So goes the saying in many parts of Europe.

A sheaf of wheat is tied with a wide red plastic ribbon bow and attached to the bird feeder by the window. The birds will enjoy the tiny kernels in the wheat as well as the food on the feeder, and you'll have the joy of watching them.

## BRANCHES FOR THE BIRDS

Under the window, and just beside the feeder that carries the birds' Christmas tree, attach a few sprays of balsam, yew, or hemlock for the birds to land on before approaching the feeder. A few pine cones wired to the branches add to the design and also give added perches for the birds.

☆

CHAPTER VIII

# MOBILES

The changing pattern, the quiet motion, the freely floating forms—these are the qualities that intrigue us and inspire us to make mobiles. Not only do we create a design that pleases us in all its phases, we make visible that which is invisible—the air currents come alive; their direction can be seen, and their tempo changes can be watched as the mobile moves with quiet grace or dances round and round.

Mobiles should be made so that the various sections will not touch, no matter how they move. And the real trick of making a mobile is in the balancing. Always start at the bottom and work toward the top, balancing each section as you go along. The "bottom" of the mobile is the lowest crossarm or supporting piece, not necessarily the shape that hangs down the lowest. This is shown in the photograph of the bell mobile.

## BELL MOBILE

For this mobile you will need six bells, three pieces of 16-gauge wire (either copper, which is very pliable and easy to use, or regular iron wire), black thread, and glue. The wires are 3 inches, 5 inches, and 7 inches long.

The bells are made of half circles of metallic foil stapled to form cones. Black thread is attached inside the bell with a touch of glue.

With long-nosed pliers, make an "eye," turning it under, at each end of the three pieces of wire—don't quite close the eyes. Attach a bell by its thread to each end of the shortest wire, knotting the thread and securing it and smoothing it with a touch of glue. With the pliers, close the wire eye as tight as you can.

I always find the balance point of each section of a mobile by placing the wire across my finger, as shown in the photograph. Because the bells are the same size, the balance point of this bottom section of the mobile should be the center of the wire. At the balance point, make a loop in the wire, turning it upward. I like to use my hands for this, but you may find it easier to use pliers. After making the loop at the balance point, carefully straighten out the crossarm so that it runs in a slight curve from one bell to the other, keeping both eyes and the balance-point loop parallel.

Run a thread through the loop at the balance point, and hold up the bottom

137

section of your mobile to make sure it is properly balanced. The loop can be moved one way or the other with pliers to correct balance.

Attach the thread in loop of balance point to one end of the middle-sized piece of wire, knotting and gluing it securely. Leave about an inch of thread between the two wires. Tighten the eye.

Attach three bells to one thread—a bit of glue will hold them—and hang the cluster to the other end of the second piece of wire. Knot the thread, secure with glue, and tighten the eye.

Then find the balance point of the two sections of your mobile by suspend-

ing across your finger. At the balance point turn a loop upward, attach thread, hold up to see that it is in balance, and attach to one end of the longest piece of wire. Attach the last bell to the other end of the top wire, find balance point, turn a loop, attach a thread—and your mobile is completed.

## ANGEL MOBILE

A three-piece mobile is one of the simplest to make. These three angels float freely in space, each one seemingly independent of the others and yet maintaining a relationship to the others.

Besides the three angels, you will need two 8-inch pieces of 16-gauge wire, black thread, and glue. For instructions on making the angels, see the chapter on decorations that hang.

Make "eyes" in each end of the two pieces of wire, as for the bell mobile. Attach an angel to each end of one wire, using a shorter thread for one so that it will hang higher than the other. Because the angels are the same size, the balance point of this bottom section should be in the middle of the wire crossarm. Make a loop at the balance point, attach a thread, and then fasten the thread to one end of the second

piece of wire. Attach the third angel to the other end of the second wire, and place crossarm across your finger to find the balance point of the entire mobile. Turn a loop at that point and run a thread through it and suspend the mobile.

## BIRD MOBILE

Four feathered friends fly by, as the fifth comes circling back. Birds are excellent for mobiles as the air is their natural element and they seem right at home. And five is a good number—it gives an asymmetrical configuration.

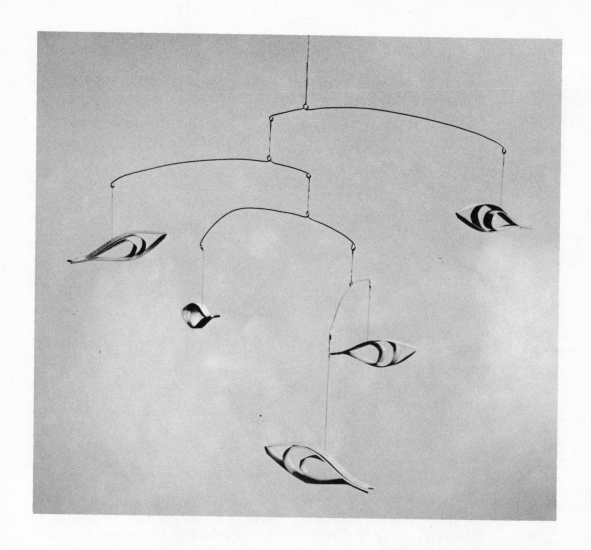

This mobile takes four pieces of wire, the bottom one 7 inches long. Each succeeding wire is ½ inch longer than the one below it—so that you need wires 7, 7½, 8, and 8½ inches long.

Proceed exactly as with the angel mobile, adding two more wires and two more birds. For instructions on making the birds, see the chapter on decorations that hang.

This mobile moves easily with the slightest air current because the wings provide fairly large surfaces to catch the air. Use two colors, perhaps blue for the bodies and yellow for the wings of three of the birds and reverse the colors for two, giving them yellow bodies and blue wings.

Your birds will never stop flying!

## FISH MOBILE

The fish mobile is designed exactly like the bird mobile. But the fish move more deliberately because they have no flat surfaces to catch the air. It almost seems as though they were swimming.

These fish are 4 inches long. Each one is made of three strips of construction paper—an 8-inch strip, a 6-inch strip, and a 5-inch strip, each ¾ inch wide. The strips are stapled together, one inside the other, notched for the tail, pointed for the nose. Each fish is suspended by a thread. (See chapter on decorations that hang.)

Use two colors (mine are blue and green) and copper wire for this one. It has more delicacy than the iron wire and somehow the fish seem to require the coppery sheen.

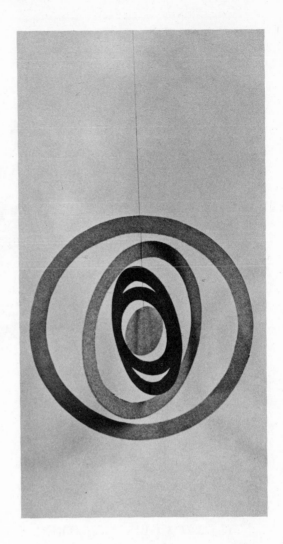

## RINGS FROM OUTER SPACE

Mobile greeting cards are fun to make for your special friends. Here a series of circles twirl one within the other, like something from outer space.

### Start with a Circle

On a sheet of bright red construction paper, draw nine circles, one outside the next, graduated in size. Use the same central point and these diameters: 1 inch, 1½ inches; 2½ inches; 3 inches; 4 inches; 4½ inches; 5½ inches; 6 inches; and finally, for the largest circle, use a diameter of 7 inches. (If you use a compass and if you set your compass with a ruler, use *half* these measurements, because you will be measuring the *radius*.)

After all nine circles are drawn, cut on every line. You will end up with four rings, each ½ inch wide, and a center-piece an inch across. (You will also, of course, have four rings, each ¼ inch wide, but discard these.)

Arrange the rings within each other, placing the center circle exactly in the middle. Put a dab of glue along one radius, starting at the center point and going to the outer edge. Along this line of glue, place a thread of matching color, leaving plenty of thread with which to hang the mobile. It will dry in a moment. Write your holiday greeting on the center circle.

## STYLIZED CHRISTMAS TREE

A mobile Christmas card in the shape of a stylized tree is made from a triangle of green construction paper.

### Start with a Triangle

Cut a triangle 7 inches by 7 inches by 6 inches, with the shortest side forming the base of the tree. Inside this triangle, draw another 5½ inches by 5½ inches by 4½ inches, and then another one 5 inches by 5 inches by 4 inches; then one 3½ inches by 3½ inches by 2¼ inches; and finally a triangle 2¾ inches by 2¾

inches by 2¼ inches. Cut on all lines and you will have three "trees" to suspend, one within the other. The center triangle is solid.

Arrange the triangles carefully, with the center one exactly in the middle. From the top point of the center triangle, run a matching thread with a bit of glue on it up through the points of the other two triangles, leaving a long piece to hang the mobile by.

As the mobile moves, the "tree" becomes three-dimensional. Write a Christmas message on the center triangle—and mail the mobile.

## CHRISTMAS-TREE MOBILE

Here's another mobile that can be used for a greeting card.

### Start with a Triangle

Out of green construction paper, cut a triangle 6 inches by 6 inches by 8 inches, with the 8 inches forming the base. This will give you a short and squatty triangle. Starting at the bottom, cut it into strips ¾ inch wide. The point at the top will be 1½ inches deep. Cut a tapered piece for the pot the tree appears to be standing in—a piece about

1½ inches high, 2 inches across the top, and 1¼ across the bottom.

Arrange the pieces carefully on a newspaper, placing the strips about ½ inch apart. Run a thread from the bottom to the top, through the center of each piece, and fasten with glue. Be very sure your thread is in the exact center of each piece or your tree mobile will be lopsided. Leave plenty of thread at top to use for hanging the mobile.

Cut matching triangles, if you like, or triangles of different colors, and run the thread between them. I like to alternate the colors—one red strip, then one green, then another red one.

## STANDING MOBILE

This Christmas-ball mobile, 12 inches high, makes a charming conversation piece for your coffee table.

Proceed step by step from the bottom to the top. Use tiny Christmas balls, four that measure ½ inch in diameter and five measuring 1 inch in diameter. Use one color or perhaps two—no more. Mine is gold and green.

No thread is used for this mobile, except at the top, so that it moves as a unit. The balls are attached to the wire crossbars by their wire loops.

You will need eight pieces of 18-gauge wire: two 2½-inch pieces, four 3-inch pieces, and two 4-inch pieces.

Starting at the bottom, attach ½-inch balls to each end of a 2½-inch piece of wire (first making an "eye" at the ends of the wires with long-nosed pliers). Turn a loop at the balance point (which will be the center, as the balls are the same size), and to this loop attach one end of a 3-inch piece of wire. At the other end attach a 1-inch ball. Find the

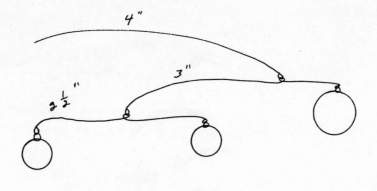

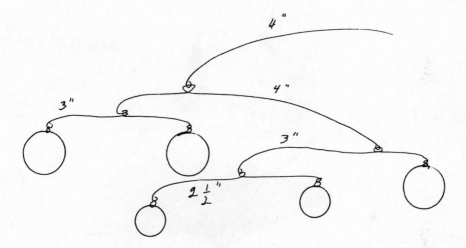

balance point, turn a loop, and attach a 4-inch piece of wire. Your mobile now looks like the first sketch.

Next, attach 1-inch balls to each end of a 3-inch wire, turn a loop at the balance point (the center this time), and attach this unit to the other end of the 4-inch wire. Turn a loop at the balance point, and to this loop attach one end of a 4-inch wire. Your mobile now looks like the second sketch.

To the other end of this 4-inch wire, attach a unit of 1-inch balls on a 3-inch wire. Again find a balance point.

You now have two wires and two balls left to use. Attach one end of the 3-inch wire remaining to the balance-point loop of the preceding 4-inch piece, and to the other end attach a unit of 1-inch balls on the remaining 2½-inch wire—this unit is just like the one you started with.

Find the balance point of the very top crossbar, turn a loop, and suspend your mobile by a small loop of thread. Hang on a table standard, leaving 1½ inches between the top of the mobile and the hook of the standard.

## STANDARD FOR THE
## TABLE MOBILE

The standard for the standing mobile has a wooden base, 3½ inches by 4½ inches, cut from ½-inch plywood and painted black. The bracket is made of 10-gauge brass wire (this is 1/16 inch thick) curved in a semicircle. A loop at the top holds the mobile. The bottom ¼ inch of the wire is bent at a right angle and fitted into a 1/16-inch hole drilled in the base about 1 inch in from the shorter edge.

When Christmas is over and your mobile is packed away for another season, use the standard for another mobile—perhaps an abstract one of your own design. Or make one of a spade, a heart, a diamond, and a club, and use it for your next bridge party.

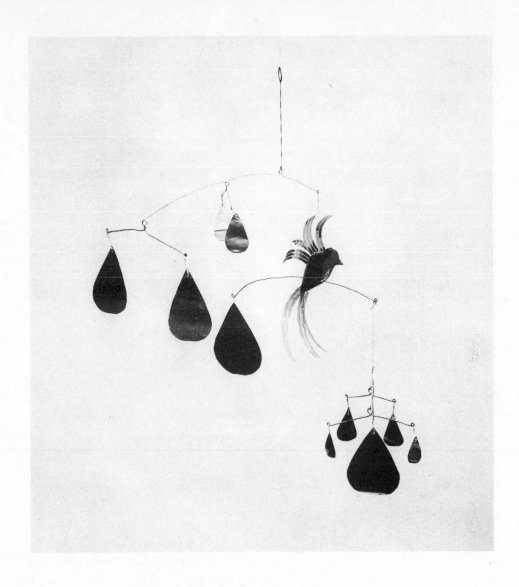

## PEAR-TREE MOBILE

The pear-tree mobile, with its partridge perched on the center wire, is made of very thin copper sheeting. The bird is made of metallic foil according to instructions given for the partridge in the espalier tree, in the chapter on tables and trees.

The design of the mobile is more complex, but it is made in the same way as the simpler ones—starting at the bottom, each section is balanced as one proceeds toward the top. Use 18-gauge wire, and try your own design. Coat the "pears" and the wires with clear lacquer (or clear nail polish) to prevent tarnishing.

## CHRISTMAS FANTASIA

Gold and silver metallic-foil fringe was used for a sort of mobile fantasia.

Cut small pieces of metallic-foil fringe about 1 inch long, reverse one piece, and weave the fringe together, as shown in photograph. Place a piece of black thread between the two pieces and fasten with glue. This makes the top of the three forms of the mobile, a sort of cap by which to suspend the form.

The bottom part of the bell forms (center and left in photograph) are made of 3-inch sections of fringe woven together and glued inside the "cap."

For the feathery form at the right (top), glue 3-inch woven pieces inside the cap as with the bell shapes. Then add at each side 1-inch pieces woven together, placing them at right angles to the cap.

Attach the threads to wire crossbars 6 inches long, balancing each section as you go along—from the bottom to the top. Make the threads of different lengths so each shape will hang at a different level—about 2 inches apart.

The foil catches the light as it catches the air, so that it glitters as it moves.

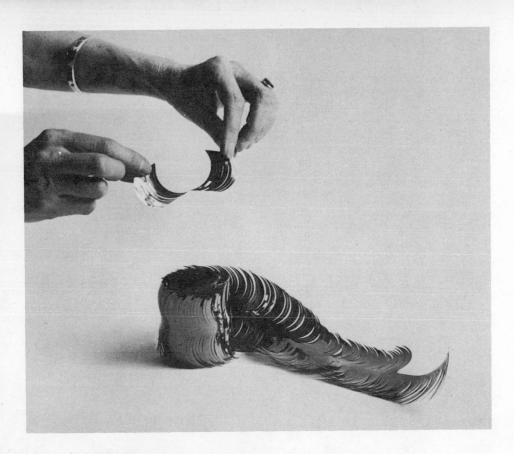

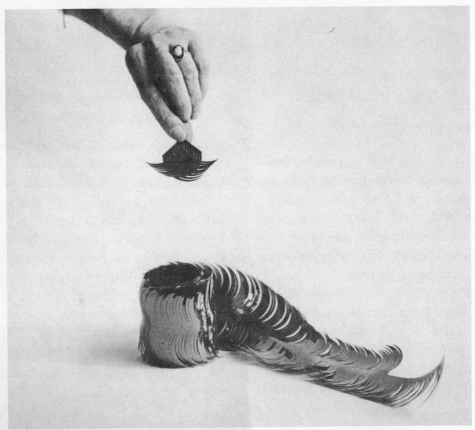

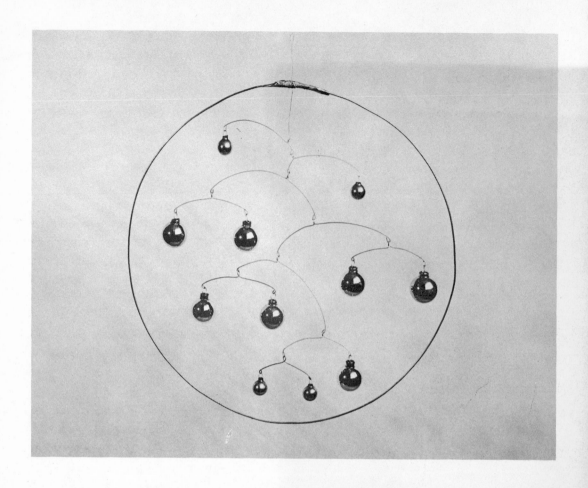

## THE GOLDEN CIRCLE

Christmas-tree balls in a circle of gold
—this mobile hangs parallel with the
wall and is 12 inches in diameter.

You will need four Christmas-tree
balls ½ inch in diameter and seven balls
1 inch in diameter. Use one color or perhaps two, but no more.

Cut ten pieces of 16-gauge wire in
these sizes: two 2-inch pieces, five 4-inch
pieces, and three 6-inch pieces. Cover
each wire with gold paint.

Start at the bottom and balance each
section as you go along. No thread is
used, the balls being attached by their
wire loops. (See drawings on page 152.)

1. Attach ½-inch balls to each end of
a 3-inch wire (using long-nosed pliers
to make a loop at each end of the wire).
Turn a loop at the balance point (see
photograph for the bell mobile). This
time the balance point will be in the
center of the arm because the balls are
the same size. With pliers, give the loop
a quarter turn so that it sits at right angles to the wire crossarm, as shown in
sketch. (Every balance-point loop in
this mobile is turned at right angles to
the wire arm. This keeps the mobile in
one plane.)

2. To this balance-point loop, attach one end of a 4-inch wire (again using pliers). To the other end of the 4-inch wire, attach a 1-inch ball.

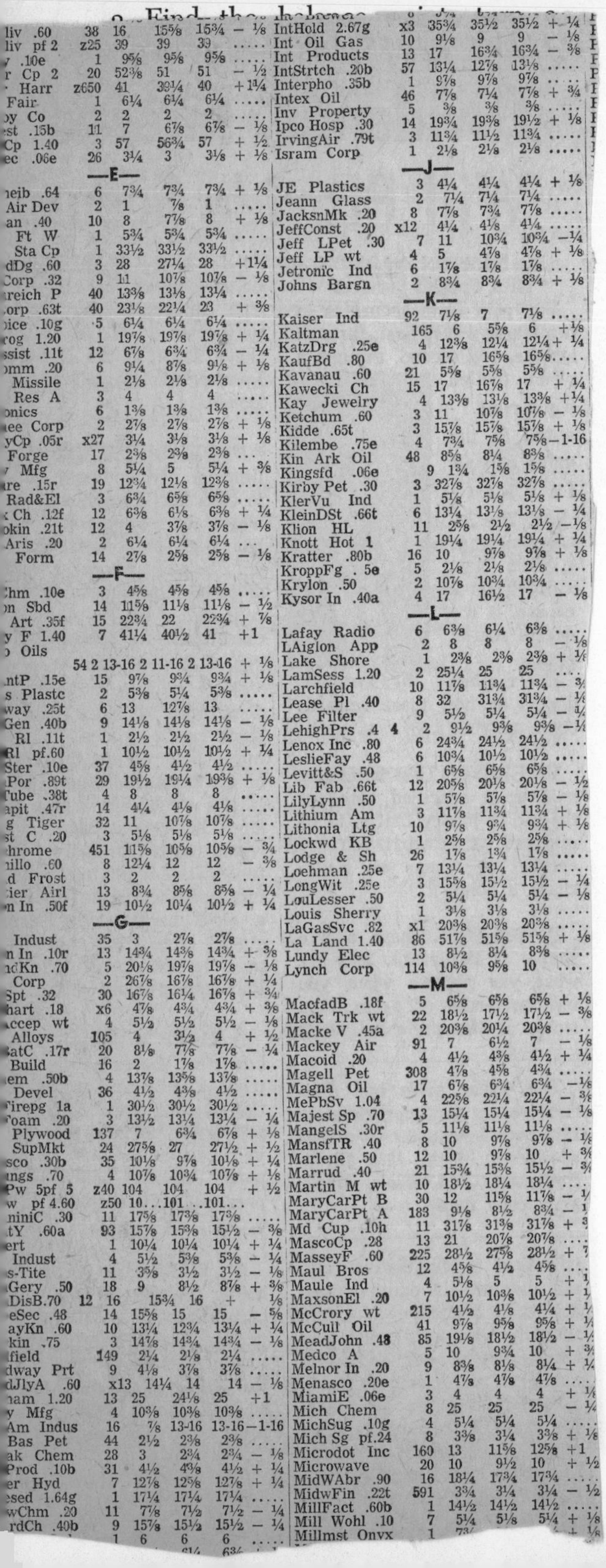

3. Find the balance...

tach a 1-inch ball. Turn loop at balance point (the center) and give loop a quarter turn. Attach this unit to end of 6-inch wire in step number 10.

12. Find the balance point, turn a loop, and give it a quarter turn.

13. To this loop, attach the last 4-inch wire, in the opposite direction.

14. To the other end of the 4-inch wire, attach a ½-inch ball.

15. Find the balance point, turn a loop, and give it a quarter turn.

16. To this loop, attach in opposite direction the *last* wire (3-inch), and attach a ½-inch ball to the other end.

17. Find balance point. Put a very fine wire through the balance-point loop —and this time don't bother with the quarter turn.

For the golden circle you will need a piece of 10-gauge wire 41 inches long. Form a circle, overlapping ends of wire and securing with masking tape. Paint the circle gold. This will give you a circle 12 inches in diameter.

Suspend the mobile inside the circle. It should just about fill the space. Hang from a wall bracket.

---

```
liv .60        38    16      15⅝    15¾   - ⅛
liv pf 2      z25    39      39     39    .....
y .10e          1     9⅝      9⅝     9⅝   .....
r Cp 2         20    52⅜     51     51    - ½
Harr         z650    41      39¼    40    +1¼
Fair            1     6¼      6¼     6¼   .....
by Co           2     2       2      2    .....
st .15b        11     7       6⅞     6⅞   - ⅛
Cp 1.40         3    57      56¾    57    + ½
ec .05e        26     3¼      3      3⅛   + ⅛

----- E -----
neib .64        6     7¾      7¾     7¾   + ⅛
Air Dev         1             ⅞      1    .....
an .40         10     8       7⅞     8    + ⅛
Ft W            1     5¾      5¾     5¾   .....
Sta Cp          1    33½     33½    33½   .....
dDg .60         3    28      27¼    28    +1¼
Corp .32        9    11      10⅞    10⅞   - ⅛
ureich P       40    13⅜     13⅛    13¼   .....
orp .63t       40    23⅛     22⅞    23    + ⅜
ice .10g        .5    6¼      6¼     6¼   .....
rog 1.20        1    19⅜     19⅞    19⅜   + ¼
ssist .11t     12     6⅞      6¾     6¾   - ¼
mm .20          6     9¼      8⅞     9⅛   + ⅛
Missile         1     2⅛      2⅛     2⅛   .....
Res A           3     4       4      4    .....
onics           6     1⅜      1⅜     1⅜   .....
ee Corp         2     2⅞      2⅞     2⅞   + ⅛
yCp .05r      x27     3¼      3⅛     3⅛   + ⅛
Forge          17     2⅜      2⅜     2⅜   .....
Mfg             8     5¼      5      5¼   + ⅜
are .15r       19    12¾     12⅛    12⅜   .....
Rad&El          3     6¾      6⅝     6⅝   .....
Ch .12f        12     6⅜      6¼     6⅜   + ¼
okin .21t      12     4       3⅞     3⅞   - ⅛
Aris .20        2     6¼      6¼     6¼   .....
Form           14     2⅞      2⅝     2⅝   - ⅛

----- F -----
hm .10e         3     4⅝      4⅝     4⅝   .....
n Sbd           1    11⅜     11⅛    11⅜   - ¼
Art .35f       15    22¾     22     22¾   + ⅞
y F 1.40        7    41¼     40½    41    +1
Oils           54  2 13-16  2 11-16  2 13-16  + ⅛
ntP .15e       15     9⅞      9¾     9¾   - ⅛
s Plastc        2     5⅝      5¼     5⅝   .....
way .25t        6    13      12⅞    13    .....
Gen .40b        9    14⅛     14⅛    14⅛   - ⅛
Rl .11t         1     2½      2½     2½   - ⅛
Rl pf.60        1    10½     10½    10½   + ¼
Ster .10e      37     4⅝      4½     4½   .....
Por .89t       29    19½     19¼    19⅜   + ⅛
ube .38t        4     8       8      8    .....
apit .47r      14     4¼      4⅛     4⅛   .....
g Tiger        32    11      10⅞    10⅞   .....
st C .20        3     5⅛      5⅛     5⅛   .....
hrome         451    11⅜     10⅝    10⅝   - ¾
illo .60        8    12¼     12     12    - ⅜
d Frost         3     2       2      2    .....
ier Airl       13     8¾      8⅝     8⅝   - ¼
n In .50f      19    10½     10¼    10½   + ¼

----- G -----
Indust         35     3       2⅞     2⅞   .....
n In .10r      13    14¾     14⅜    14¾   + ⅜
dKn .70         5    20⅛     19⅞    19⅞   - ⅛
Corp            2    26⅞     16⅞    16⅞   + ¼
Spt .32        30    16⅞     16¼    16⅞   + ¾
hart .18       x6     4⅞      4¾     4¾   + ⅜
ccep wt         4     5½      5½     5½   - ⅛
Alloys        105     4       3½     4    + ½
atC .17r       20     8½      7⅞     7⅞   - ¼
Build          16     2       1⅞     1⅞   .....
em .50b         4    13⅞     13⅝    13⅞   .....
Devel          36     4½      4⅜     4½   .....
ireqg 1a        1    30½     30½    30½   .....
oam .20         3    13½     13¼    13¼   - ¼
Plywood       137     7       6¾     6⅞   + ⅛
SupMkt         24    27⅝     27     27½   + ½
sco .30b       35    10⅛      9⅞    10⅛   + ¼
ngs .70         4    10⅞     10¾    10⅞   + ⅛
Pw 5pf 5      z40   104     104    104    .....
w pf 4.60     z50    10...101 ..101...
niniC .30      11    17⅞     17⅞    17⅞   .....
tY .60a        93    15⅞     15⅜    15½   - ⅜
ert             1    10¼     10¼    10¼   + ¼
Indust          4     5½      5⅜     5⅜   - ¼
s-Tite         11     3⅝      3½     3½   - ⅛
Gery .50       18     9       8½     8⅞   + ⅜
DisB.70        12    16      15¾    16    +
eSec .48       14    15⅝     15     15    - ⅝
ayKn .60       10    13¼     12¾    13¼   + ¼
kin .75         3    14⅞     14¾    14¾   - ⅛
field         149     2¼      2⅛     2¼   .....
LJlyA .60     x13    14¼     14     14    - ¼
nam 1.20       13    25      24⅛    25    +1
y Mfg           4    10⅜     10⅜    10⅜   .....
Am Indus       16     ⅞  13-16   13-16   -1-16
Bas Pet        44     2½      2⅜     2⅜   .....
ak Chem        28     3       2¾     2¾   - ⅛
Prod .10b      31     4½      4⅜     4½   + ¼
er Hyd          7    12⅛     12⅜    12⅜   + ¼
sed 1.64g       1    17¼     17¼    17¼   .....
wChm .20       11     7⅞      7½     7⅞   .....
rdCh .40b       9    15⅞     15½    15½   - ¼
                1     6       6      6    .....
```

```
IntHold 2.67g   x3   35¾    35½    35½   + ¼
Int Oil Gas     10    9⅛     9      9    - ⅛
Int Products    13   17     16¾    16¾   - ⅜
IntStrtch .20b  57   13¼    12⅞    13⅛   .....
Interpho .35b    1    9⅞     9⅞     9⅞   .....
Intex Oil       46    7⅞     7¼     7⅞   + ¾
Inv Property     5    ⅜      ⅜      ⅜    .....
Ipco Hosp .30   14   19⅜    19⅜    19½   + ⅛
IrvingAir .79t   3   11¾    11½    11¾   .....
Isram Corp       1    2⅛     2⅛     2⅛   .....

----- J -----
JE Plastics      3    4¼     4¼     4¼   + ⅛
Jeann Glass      2    7¼     7¼     7¼   .....
JacksnMk .20     8    7⅞     7¾     7⅞   .....
JeffConst .20  x12    4¼     4⅛     4⅛   .....
Jeff LPet .30    7   11     10¾    10¾   - ¼
Jeff LP wt       4    5      4⅞     4⅞   + ⅛
Jetronic Ind     6    1⅞     1⅞     1⅞   .....
Johns Bargn      2    8¾     8¼     8¼   + ⅛

----- K -----
Kaiser Ind      92    7⅛     7      7⅛   .....
Kaltman        165    6      5⅝     6    + ⅝
KatzDrg .25e     4   12⅜    12¼    12¼   + ¼
KaufBd .80      10   17     16⅝    16⅝   .....
Kavanau .60     21    5⅝     5⅝     5⅝   .....
Kawecki Ch      15   17     16⅞    17    + ¼
Kay Jewelry      4   13⅜    13⅛    13⅜   + ¼
Ketchum .60      3   11     10⅞    10⅞   - ⅛
Kidde .65t       3   15⅞    15⅝    15⅞   + ⅛
Kilembe .75e     4    7¾     7⅝     7⅝   -1-16
Kin Ark Oil     48    8⅝     8¼     8⅝   .....
Kingsfd .06e     9    1¾     1⅝     1⅝   .....
Kirby Pet .30    3   32⅞    32⅛    32⅞   .....
KlerVu Ind       1    5⅛     5⅛     5⅛   + ⅛
KleinDSt .66t    6   13¼    13⅛    13⅛   - ¼
Klion HL        11    2⅝     2½     2½   - ⅛
Knott Hot 1      1   19¼    19¼    19¼   + ¼
Kratter .80b    16   10      9⅞     9⅞   + ⅛
KroppFg . 5e     5    2⅛     2⅛     2⅛   .....
Krylon .50       2   10⅞    10¾    10¾   .....
Kysor In .40a    4   17     16½    17    - ⅛

----- L -----
Lafay Radio      6    6⅜     6¼     6⅜   .....
LAiglon App      2    8      8      8    - ⅛
Lake Shore       1    2⅜     2⅜     2⅜   + ½
LamSess 1.20     2   25¼    25     25    .....
Larchfield      10   11⅞    11¾    11¾   - ⅜
Lease Pl .40     8   32     31¾    31¾   - ¼
Lee Filter       9    5½     5¼     5¼   - ¼
LehighPrs .4     2    9½     9⅜     9⅜   -1⅛
Lenox Inc .80    6   24¾    24½    24½   .....
LeslieFay .48    6   10¾    10½    10½   .....
Levitt&S .50     1    6⅛     6⅝     6⅝   .....
Lib Fab .66t    12   20⅝    20⅛    20⅛   - ½
LilyLynn .50     1    5⅞     5⅞     5⅞   - ⅛
Lithium Am       3   11⅞    11¾    11¾   + ⅛
Lithonia Ltg    10    9⅞     9⅞     9¾   + ⅛
Lockwd KB        1    2⅝     2⅝     2⅝   .....
Lodge & Sh      26    1⅞     1¾     1⅞   .....
Loehman .25e     7   13¼    13¼    13¼   .....
LongWit .25e     3   15⅞    15½    15½   - ¼
LouLesser .50    2    5¼     5¼     5¼   - ⅛
Louis Sherry     1    3⅛     3⅛     3⅛   .....
LaGasSvc .82    x1   20⅜    20⅜    20⅜   .....
La Land 1.40    86   51⅞    51⅝    51⅝   + ⅛
Lundy Elec      13    8½     8¼     8⅜   .....
Lynch Corp     114   10⅜     9⅝    10    .....

----- M -----
MacfadB .18f     5    6⅝     6⅝     6⅝   + ⅛
Mack Trk wt     22   18½    17½    17½   - ⅜
Macke V .45a     2   20⅜    20¼    20⅜   .....
Mackey Air      91    7      6½     7    - ⅛
Macoid .20       4    4½     4⅜     4½   + ¼
Magell Pet     308    4⅞     4⅝     4¾   .....
Magna Oil       17    6⅞     6¾     6¾   - ⅛
MePbSv 1.04      4   22⅝    22¼    22¼   - ⅜
Majest Sp .70   13   15¼    15¼    15¼   - ⅛
MangelS .30r     5   11⅛    11⅛    11⅛   .....
MansfTR .40      8   10      9⅞     9⅞   - ⅛
Marlene .50     12   10      9⅞    10    + ¾
Marrud .40      21   15¾    15⅝    15½   - ⅜
Martin M wt     10   18½    18¼    18¼   .....
MaryCarPt B     30   12     11⅝    11⅞   - ½
MaryCarPt A    183    9¼     8½     8¾   - ⅛
Md Cup .10h     11   31⅞    31⅜    31⅞   + ¾
MascoCp .28     13   21     20⅞    20⅞   .....
MasseyF .60    225   28½    27⅝    28½   + ¾
Maul Bros       12    4⅜     4¼     4⅜   .....
Maule Ind        4    5⅛     5      5    + ⅛
MaxsonEl .20     7   10½    10⅜    10½   + ¼
McCrory wt     215    4½     4⅛     4¼   + ⅛
McCull Oil      41    9⅞     9⅝     9⅝   - ⅛
MeadJohn .48    85   19⅛    18½    18½   - ¼
Medco A          5   10      9¾    10    + ⅜
Melnor In .20    9    8⅜     8⅛     8¼   + ⅛
Menasco .20      1    4⅞     4¾     4⅞   .....
MiamiE .06e      3    4      4      4    + ⅛
Mich Chem        8   25     25     25    - ¼
MichSug .10g     4    5¼     5¼     5¼   .....
Mich Sg pf.24    8    3⅜     3¼     3⅜   + ⅛
Microdot Inc   160   13     11⅝    12⅝   +1
Microwave       20   10      9½    10    + ¼
MidWAbr .90     16   18¼    17¾    17¾   .....
MidwFin .22t   591    3¾     3¼     3¼   .....
MillFact .60b    1   14½    14½    14½   .....
Mill Wohl .10    7    5¼     5⅛     5⅛   - ⅛
Millmst Onyx     1    7¾
```

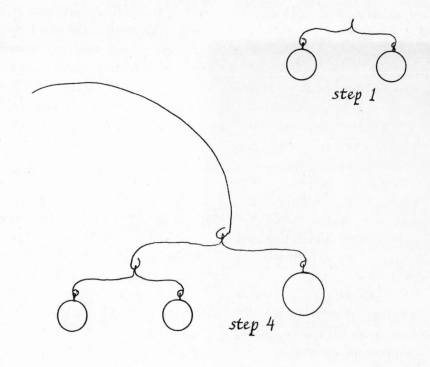

step 1

step 4

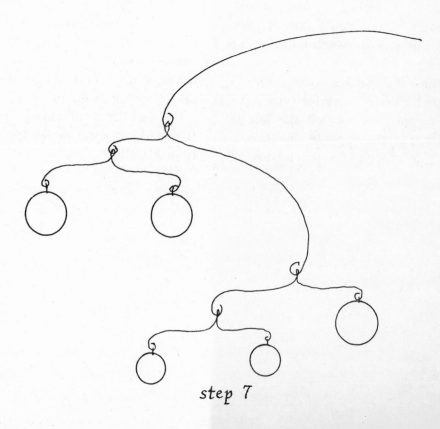

step 7

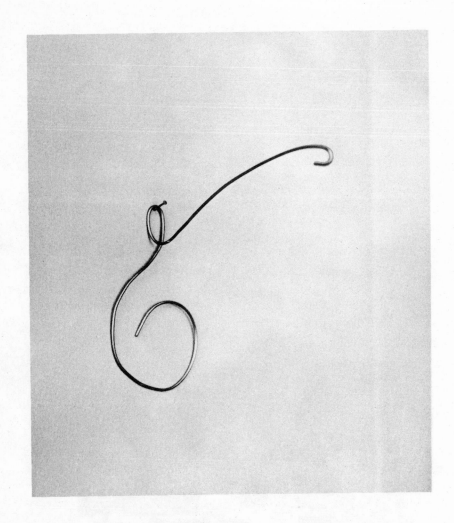

## WALL BRACKET

The wall bracket is made of a piece of 10-gauge wire 30 inches long. With pliers, shape the wire to form a sort of G-clef, as shown in photograph. Make the arm about 10 inches long. The G-clef acts as a brace against the wall for the arm. Paint it gold or silver and hang from a hook.

The bracket is useful for mobiles, candle chandeliers, and other hanging decorations.

☆

# CHAPTER IX

# WHAT DO YOU DO WITH YOUR CHRISTMAS CARDS?

What do you do with your Christmas cards? You open them joyfully, admire them extravagantly, display them prominently—and then what do you do with them? When Christmas is over and the decorations come down, do you look at the cards once more and then ruefully relegate them to the rubbish pile? Don't do it!

Your Christmas cards are treasures of more than passing fancy. Tuck them away—and remember where you put them! Next season when the snows are swirling around and Christmas is on the way, get out the scissors, ruler, and paste pot and your carefully saved treasures—last year's Christmas cards. You'll find dozens of things to do with them. Here are just a few.

## CUTOUT PLACE CARDS

Place cards for your family dinner can be made of Christmas-card cutouts.

Make them in series—trees, candles, Madonnas. For the children's table use cutouts of Santas or angels. Here is a forest of trees for a party of six.

Cut out the figures with embroidery scissors. The trick is to silhouette them completely, taking out every bit of background. For the base use colored construction paper or plain white bond, about 2 inches by 4 inches, depending on the size of the cutouts. A strip of the same paper, ¼ inch wide, is pasted to one edge of the base and then to the figure, as shown in the sketch. Paste the shaded area. Let the figure stand off-center, leaving space on the base for the dinner guest's name.

Lift the figure gently up and back, and it will stand on the base. To fold flat, tuck the base up behind the figure.

Make place cards of Madonnas, both modern and traditional. The Three Wise Men make excellent cutouts too.

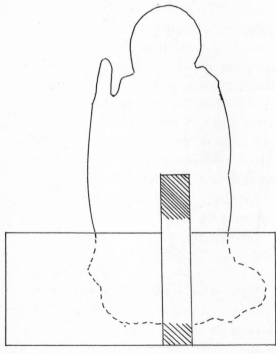

## THREE WISE MEN

These Wise Men stand about 6 inches tall and are richly colored and bright with gold. Larger cutouts such as these can be used to trim a mantel or a buffet table. Stand them on bases like the place cards.

Be sure to cut out all the background, even around the tassels on the Wise Men's caps and between their bodies, as you can see in the Wise Men on the right of the photograph, and around the points of the crowns of those at the left.

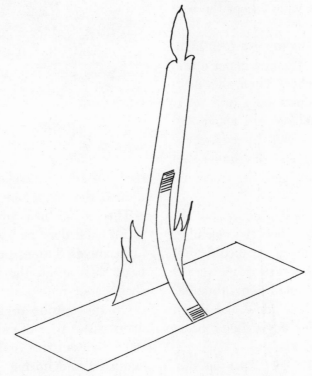

## ADVENT CALENDAR

An Advent calendar for your door—an inside door, as it won't withstand the weather—is made with Christmas cards. It's fascinating to do, and when it's finished it will add to the air of expectancy that prevails all during December.

Use brightly colored construction paper—mine is a rosy-red—6 inches wide and 32 inches long. This means that you will have to use two pieces, each 6 inches by 15 inches, and join them at the back with cellophane tape, covering the joint on the front with garlands of holly cut from Christmas cards.

First, measure and mark the twenty-four windows and doors (one for each day of December, from the first to Christmas Eve). I made windows above the center garland and doors below it, all of them 1 inch wide except the top three.

The window at the top is 1 inch high and 2 inches wide. The two under it are 1 inch by 1½ inches. Then the next three rows of windows are 1 inch by 1 inch each. The windows just above the holly garland are 1 inch by 1½ inches.

The doors in the first row under the garland are 2 inches high, the others 2½ inches high.

When the doors and windows are all drawn with pencil, place the calendar on a board or a heavy cardboard and cut—carefully—with a razor blade across the top and bottom, and down through the middle of each window and door. Cut against a ruler edge. Bend back the shutters and doors.

Paste a strip of shelf paper on the

back of the calendar, putting paste around the edges only.

Then comes the search for tiny figures to fill each door and window! Cut out little angels, kittens, and candles, and paste them inside the shutters onto the shelf paper underneath.

On the outside of the shutters and doors paste strips of patterns in gold, or stained-glass strips from church scenes, matching and mixing as you like. You

(*page 163*)

[35] A non-melting snowman can set the mood for your holiday decorations. Instructions are given in Chapter VII.

[36] With nothing more than a few leaves of holly a Christmas scene is created around the time-to-retire candlestick. See Chapter VI.

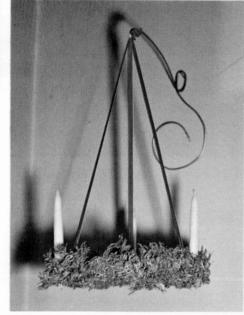

[37] A chandelier of princess pine and candles is suspended over the buffet table. See Chapter III.

[38] Very large red candles and a bouquet of evergreens and red berries give Christmas color to the old Welsh dresser. See Chapter VI.

[39] The espaliered tree bearing tiny pears and a partridge stands in a plastic flowerpot. See Chapter II.

[40] Small Christmas balls decorate the gnarled branches of high-bush blueberry. Instructions are given in Chapter VII.

[41] Branches trimmed with little red hearts are fastened in a red container. For details see Chapter VII.

[42] Tissue-paper ball tops the Christmas tree or hangs in the hallway. Complete instructions are given in Chapter V.

[43] Christmas packages with intriguing decorations and in all colors are achieved with Christmas-card cutouts. See Chapter IX.

[45] Posters of Christmas scenes are made on construction paper with cutouts. See Chapter IX.

[44] Lucia, the symbol of the season of light, carries a crown of candles in her hair. See Chapter III.

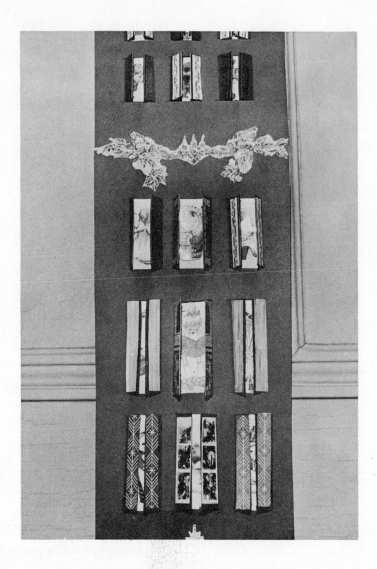

may even be lucky and find a window in your cards like the one in the center of the bottom row on mine.

The house must have a roof, of course —you'll find one somewhere among your cards. And the star of Bethlehem shines in the sky. At the bottom is the Christmas tree, set up for Christmas Eve.

Taper the top and round off the bottom, and finish off the calendar with a garland of holly like the one in the center. Open a window a day and watch the weeks go by, until it's time for Christmas.

The close-up of the Advent calendar shows the tiny figures inside the little doors—an angel singing, a little child with a muff sitting on a sled—and the patterns on the shutters. Formal Christmas cards are often edged with designs in gold and silver that can be used for this purpose.

## CHILDREN'S GAME OF CUTOUTS

Here's a game for the children's party. Give each child half a dozen cutouts already pasted to their bases. Mix them up so that each child has a variety of forms.

Give them ten minutes to set up their characters. The prize goes to the child who creates the best scene.

If you have enough cards and scissors and paste pots, and plenty of time, let the children start at the beginning, cutting out the figures and pasting them to their bases. Again, the prize goes to the best scene or the scene that tells the best story: The galloping knight is headed for the old-fashioned lady holding Christmas candy in her bowl, while the rooster stands watching and the poodle goes on tying a knot on his Christmas package.

Many candles light the manuscript the old monk is working on.

The dog with the bell on his tail offers a Christmas branch to a curious rooster.

The little Japanese lady stands and watches the Santa, the choir boy, and the snowman singing Christmas carols.

## SHELF-PAPER POSTER

In many parts of the world it is the custom to decorate the walls with colorful Christmas posters. In Scandinavia, particularly in the kitchen, bright posters are hung on the walls.

Cutouts from Christmas cards make marvelous posters. A roll of shelf paper, a pile of Christmas cards, scissors, and paste—and you won't hear a sound out of the children for the whole of a stormy day!

This one was made on a strip of white shelf paper, about 40 inches long. Part of the fun is choosing colors that go well together, and again the trick is to silhouette the figures completely. All of the candles across the bottom of the poster came from the same card.

The close-up of the shelf-paper poster shows how the cutouts can be grouped to tell stories. The candles are used as a device to separate one part of the tale from the next.

## CONSTRUCTION-PAPER POSTER

Bright blue construction paper 18 inches long and 9½ inches wide was used for the poster of the carolers. Smaller posters such as this one need only one main idea. It sometimes takes quite a search through the cards to find the right cutouts.

## CHILDREN'S PLACE CARDS

Cutouts of children are always appealing. These can be made into simple place cards that are especially good for the children's table.

Choose figures of about the same size —3 to 4 inches tall. For the base, use plain white cards 4 inches square, or use 4-inch squares of colored construction paper. Fold the square in half and paste the figure to the folded card, slightly off-center so that there will be room for the name. These place cards make colorful and attractive additions to the party table.

Make them in sets for Christmas gifts. As long as the figures are not taller than the *unfolded* cards, they will pack nicely in an envelope.

## CHRISTMAS-CARD MOBILES

Mobiles of Christmas cards carry an abundance of holiday greetings. They are intriguing to make and not as simple as they seem to be.

In the first place, you must choose cards that go well together—colors and subjects should harmonize.

In the second place, each card must have one of a matching size to back it. If you can't find just the right card for this, use a piece of colored paper or Christmas wrapping paper that has an interesting design.

You must also have variation in shapes and sizes for your mobile. The pieces at top and bottom give it form. A small sleigh bell at the bottom is a fine finishing touch—but if you want to mail your mobile for a Christmas greeting, leave off the bell.

When you have chosen your cards and the sequence in which you want them to hang, place them on a table in their proper order, with their *wrong* sides facing up. Run a black thread down the entire length of the mobile, through the center of each card. If thread is not exactly in the center of each card, the mobile will not hang properly. Add a few dabs of glue to the thread where it touches the cards, and place the matching cards on top of the thread, *right* side up. Leave enough thread at the top to make a loop for hanging.

If you have received an unusual card from a good friend, feature it in a mobile and send it back the following year!

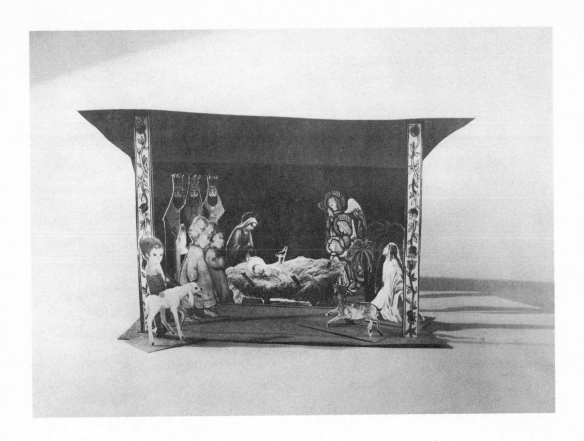

## CHRISTMAS-CARD CRECHE

The Christmas-card crèche can be made in any size you like, according to the size of your figures. I made mine of a piece of Bristol board 18 inches long and 12 inches wide. I shaped the strip as shown in the sketch on next page so that it tapered from 12 inches (across the front of the roof) to 8 inches (at the bottom of the back wall) and then widened again to 10 inches for the front edge of the floor. Fold along dotted lines. The floor is 7 inches from front to back; then the cardboard is bent up to form the back wall, which is 4½ inches high. Another bend brings the roof forward for 6½ inches.

The pillars that support the roof are strips of cardboard ½ inch wide and 8 inches long. These are glued in place inside the roof. Then, instead of gluing the other ends of the pillars to the floor, I made ½-inch slits at the places where the pillars should stand, bent the last ½ inch of the pillars, and slipped them through the slits. This makes it possible to fold the crèche flat and store it away for another year.

The pillars are decorated with designs cut from a Christmas card. The figures in the crèche are Christmas-card cutouts fastened to bases just as the place cards are. The side view of the crèche shows how the figures are grouped, some at the back and some in front, to create the Nativity scene.

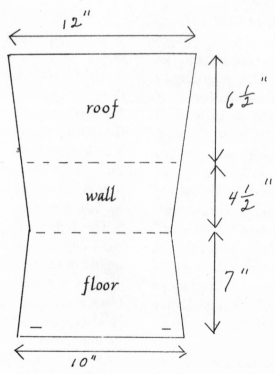

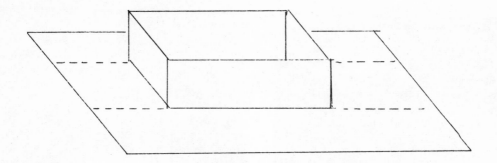

## CHRISTMAS WRAPPINGS

All those pretty packages piled high around the Christmas tree are trimmed with colors carefully chosen and ribbons tied just *so*. Finally, it is time for the family to gather round the tree, and the annual package-opening ceremony begins. Moments later the pretty packages have vanished. Piles of crumpled paper and strands of torn-up bows fill the floor.

You can keep your package pretty and open it too if you wrap the box and its cover separately. Cut a piece of paper large enough to cover the bottom part of the box and to go down ½ inch inside it. Place box in the center of the paper, snip paper to each corner of the box (see sketch), and fasten with glue. Then put wrapping paper on the cover in the same fashion, fastening paper ½ inch up inside the cover.

Decorate the cover and tie up the box—or use cellophane tape to keep the cover on. When the time comes to open the package, snip ribbon or tape and keep your decorations intact.

## DECORATE WITH CUTOUTS

Christmas-card cutouts can add to the fun of decorating your packages. Choose cutouts to suit the gift or the one to whom it goes. For instance, if the package contains a book, cut out all the candles you can find and create a design on the cover of the box to light the reader's way. Run ribbon across two corners and tie at the back of the package.

Birds that sit and birds that stand, birds flying and perching, singing and walking—collect them all to trim gifts for your friends who watch the birds.

Narrow strips of gold-colored sticky tape serve two purposes—they define the design and hold the cover on the box. Three snips of the scissors and the cover lifts off without destroying the design.

The long and narrow box seems to be made for three pink angels separated by gold cord and two simple bows. The box is wrapped in green foil.

The green and gold of the Madonna and the other figures in this religious scene are carried out in the gold wrapping and green satin ribbon.

A big package for a tiny tot is trimmed with a cageful of kiddies coming down the hill, to be met by Grandpa below.

Strips of gold-colored cellophane tape placed around the package separate the cutouts, forming the cage, and also keep the cover on. Snip the tape to open the box.

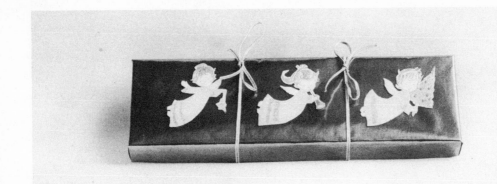

☆

CHAPTER X

# CHRISTMAS JEWELRY

Favors for your holiday party? Make some Christmas jewelry! For gifts for family and friends, for your own party dress, for a change from the Christmas corsage—make some jewelry.

Christmas jewelry is festive, it's frivolous, and it's expendable. It's simple or complicated, as you choose, and it has glitter or a sheen, depending on the material you use. Here are a few ideas to start you off.

## EARRINGS

All kinds of fascinating earrings can be made of simple materials, most of which you probably have in the house. You will need gold paint, gold cord, and glue; scissors and a small paint brush; cranberries and nuts and evergreen twigs; clear lacquer, fine wire, lace doilies, and foil. And, of course, several pairs of earring backs from your local dime store or craft shop.

Evergreen twigs are painted gold and

tied with tiny gold bows. Hazelnuts and almonds, painted gold, are hung on a cord and trimmed with bits of gilded evergreen and red satin bows. (I made holes in the nuts by piercing them with a heated icepick.)

Cranberries will last for a few weeks if they are covered with lacquer or clear nail polish. Glue them to circles of lace-paper doilies or holly-leaf shapes of green metallic foil. If you want to use cranberries in a cluster, give them a stem of very fine wire and twist the stems together.

## PINS OF PLANT MATERIALS

Pins made of plant materials last indefinitely. The end of a juniper branch (be sure it has berries on it) about 3 inches long can be sprayed or brushed with gold paint and glued to a pin back (also available at the dime store and the craft shop).

One spray of long-needled pine

painted gold has three tiny Christmas balls glued to it. Use whatever color will go with your costume. Pin is attached with glue.

A small branch painted gold holds a tiny wooden bird. These small birds usually have a sharp pin that can hold

them to a branch, but add a dab of glue to make sure they won't fall off. Attach pin to branch.

The interesting shapes of blueberry twigs make fascinating pins. Paint them in colors or gold and attach pin to the side of the twig that is the flattest.

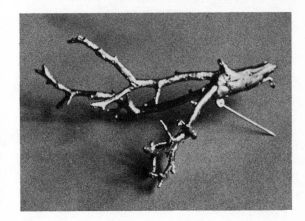

## COPPER PINS

Shapes of all kinds can be cut from copper sheeting—an angel, a bird, a Swedish star, a bell, a candle, a five-pointed star, and a holly leaf are shown here. Sparkle the pins by brushing them with glue and shaking on the glitter. Add a few sequins, as shown on the five-pointed star. The candle sits on a holly leaf—I used red glitter on the candle, gold for the flame, and green for the leaf.

The angel's wings can be bent forward and curved. The straight strips (see sketch) between the points of the Swedish star are rolled to the center. The bell is covered with gold glitter, the bottom edge outlined in red.

Pins are attached to the copper with liquid solder.

## BUTTERFLIES AND BOWS

Butterflies of brightly colored metallic foil can be glued to pins. Put glitter on the body if you like, and make the butterfly large or small—follow the pattern given. Two sets of wings are used. Bend up the lower wings to give the butterfly three dimensions, and perch him on your shoulder.

For a pin of more traditional design, use ribbons and bells. Here loops of green satin ribbon carry three silvery bells. Cut three pieces of ribbon, one 5 inches long, one 4 inches long, and one 3 inches long. Slip a bell on each piece, double the ribbons, and glue in a row on a pin. This lets the bells hang down from the pin 2½ inches, 2 inches, and 1½ inches. Cover the pin with a flat bow attached with glue.

The pin makes a pleasant jingle!

## PINS OF ALUMINUM

Aluminum pins can be made in all shapes too. Use the scraps left from your aluminum sconces.

A maple leaf, a dogwood blossom and a philodendron leaf—easy patterns to make and quite simple to cut. Smooth the edges with fine sandpaper. Gently tap the pattern on the pins with a wide screwdriver or a sharp-edged piece of wood and a hammer. Polish with extra-fine steel wool. Attach pins with liquid solder.

Aluminum cut in the shape of a Christmas tree is covered with gold glitter and dotted with red and green glitter to give the effect of Christmas balls.

An aluminum crescent is studded with golden glitter. Make the crescent as slim as you can without letting the pin on the back show.

# SOURCES FOR MATERIALS

Simple materials, easy to find, are the best ones to use for making decorations.

Paper of all sorts and colors and in many different sizes is available in dime stores, art-supply shops, and handcraft shops.

Construction paper comes in packages of fifty sheets of assorted colors, 12 inches by 18 inches, for about a dollar, or thirty-six sheets 9 inches by 12 inches for twenty-nine cents.

*Metallic foil is sold in packages of assorted colors, usually silver on one side, six 9-inch by 12-inch sheets to a package, for less than seventy-five cents.

Tissue paper, 12 inches by 18 inches, in every color of the rainbow, is available in packages of 50 sheets for about a dollar.

Bristol board you'll find in your local art-supply shop in sheets of varying sizes and colors, sold by the sheet.

Crepe paper and Christmas wrapping paper, of course, are sold in every dime store.

Typing paper, or plain white bond, comes in small packages in dime stores and stationery shops.

Many different kinds of glue are available. I've found Sobo and Elmer's the best for paper, foil, felt, and such things. Le Page's liquid solder works very well with copper and aluminum. All of these are sold in dime stores and in most hardware stores.

*Aluminum comes in 36-inch-square sheets for about four dollars at all hardware stores. One sheet is enough to make several sconces, several angels, and plenty of pins. There will probably be enough left over to make a tray for your house plants. Bend up the sides, fold the corners (do not cut or the tray will not hold water), put pebbles in the bottom, and place the potted plants on the pebbles. Keep water level just below top of the pebbles. Plants will thrive.

*Copper is sold by the sheet in handcraft shops. It comes in various thicknesses, in sheets about 15 inches square for about two dollars. I used 36-gauge for most of my decorations.

* If unavailable locally, try: American Handicraft Co. P.O. Box 791, Fort Worth, Texas

Glitter in gold and silver and in many colors comes in small bottles—sometimes with a shaker top. It also comes in tubes already mixed with glue. Hardware shops, dime stores, and art-supply shops have it.

**Oasis is sold in most florist shops. It is a foam-like material that comes in blocks and can be cut to fit your container. Soaked with water, it will keep flowers and greens fresh for many days. If you can't find floral clay at your florist shop, use plastic modeling clay, available in dime stores and hobby shops.

Small bottles of paint of all colors and gold and silver are now easy to find. Hardware stores, hobby shops, and art-supply stores have them, and also the spray paints.

Felt is sold by the yard in all fabric departments. It is usually quite wide (54 inches or more) and costs about a dollar per yard. Gold braid and cord are sold in all notion departments and shops for a few cents a yard.

Cellophane tape is available at all dime stores, stationery stores, and hardware stores. In addition to the transparent kind, it comes in many colors and patterns, particularly at Christmas time.

Double-faced cellophane tape is now available and is very useful in holding two surfaces together, especially when you don't want to use glue.

** If unavailable locally try: Smithers-Oasis Co. Kent, Ohio

A new variety of cellophane tape is the so-called invisible kind—and it actually is invisible. It is cloudy-looking on the roll, instead of being clearly transparent.

Your hardware store will supply you with wire in whatever gauge you want, in small amounts or large. It comes on cards in 6-foot lengths (both copper and regular iron wire) for a few pennies. Hardware stores also have the spool wire, which is almost as fine as thread. Silica gel is sold in some florist shops. It is a drying agent used in preparing plant material for permanent arrangements. If you can't find it locally, try one of the following mail order houses:

W. Atlee Burpee Co.
Philadelphia 32, Penna.

The Flower Dri Division of Plantabbs Corp.
Timonium, Md.

Sim Savage
So. Berwick 5, Maine

Plaster of Paris you will find in hardware and paint shops. You can buy more than you'll need for twenty-five cents.

Go to your local hobby shop or dime store for artificial fruits and leaves, for plastic ribbon, for embroidery hoops, and for Styrofoam in all shapes.

The tiny wooden birds from Scandinavia are usually available in department stores and craft shops. Sometimes one finds them in gift shops.

# INDEX